Praise for *Compete Smarter, Not Harder*

"In today's technology-driven, 'ready—fire—aim' business environment, competitive strategy is all too often left behind by the push to deliver the next shiny thing. Real competitive strategy is about prioritization; most important, prioritization that wins for customers, thereby winning for the business. *Compete Smarter, Not Harder* is on target with its simple steps to ensure the business prioritizes its efforts in an effective, efficient manner, and most important, excludes those things that are not within the strategy and only distract or divert the business. This book does a great job illustrating the importance of knowing where and how to compete. Bill's stories resonate and clearly illustrate those business principles that define success while pointing out the fallacies that are often employed as fact when making business decisions. Make this book part of your business education and keep it in your reference library."

—Greg Bowlin,
Strategia Global, LLC., and former–Senior Vice President and
Chief Strategy Officer for Jeppesen, Inc.

"This book delivers high-quality service to both scholars and practitioners. From a research perspective, it demonstrates step-by-step analysis of how to make strategic decisions on where or where not to compete in such a rapidly changing market as today, based on the process of screening for priorities. Meanwhile, it also provides specific solutions for a practitioner like me when it comes to making real and critical decisions.

Some traditional books about marketing or strategy are highly focused on one or few specific regions or customers. However, this book seeks for a universal solution by drilling into the core of competing in the right market, in the right part, for the right customers, with the right incentives, and with the right offering.

Therefore, the principles and tools can be utilized worldwide without boundaries, in the United States, China, and anywhere else.

The thought-provoking principles and tools is not elaborated in a traditional way. It is quite impressive that the book is filled with vivid examples and logical statements. The examples cover from literature, relevant theories, to the business world.

Making strategic decisions sometimes is so critical and highly related to the fortune of the entire organization. The book would enrich practitioners' minds by making important contribution to their understanding about what to focus and hence the quality of strategy decisions."

—**Kehai Xie,**
Senior Vice President and Chief Human Resources Officer of Peking University Founder Group Co., Ltd.

COMPETE SMARTER, NOT HARDER

COMPETE SMARTER, NOT HARDER

A Process for Developing the Right Priorities Through Strategic Thinking

---

WILLIAM PUTSIS

WILEY

Cover design: Paul McCarthy

Published by John Wiley & Sons, Inc., Hoboken, New Jersey.
Published simultaneously in Canada.

For general information about our other products and services, please contact our Customer Care
Department within the United States at (800) 762-2974, outside the United States at (317) 572-3993
or fax (317) 572-4002.

Wiley publishes in a variety of print and electronic formats and by print-on-demand. Some material
included with standard print versions of this book may not be included in e-books or in print-on-
demand. If this book refers to media such as a CD or DVD that is not included in the version you
purchased, you may download this material at http://booksupport.wiley.com. For more information
about Wiley products, visit www.wiley.com.

Library of Congress Cataloging-in-Publication Data:

Putsis, William, 1959-
  Compete smarter, not harder : a process for developing the right priorities through strategic
thinking/Dr. William Putsis.
    pages cm
  Includes index.
  ISBN 978-1-118-70871-2 (cloth); ISBN 978-1-118-74702-5 (ebk): ISBN 978-1-118-74716-2
(ebk)
  1. Strategic planning. 2. Target marketing. 3. Marketing—Management. I. Title.
  HD30.28.P8678 2013
  658.8′02—dc23

                                                                              2013016302

Printed in the United States of America

10 9 8 7 6 5 4 3 2 1

CONTENTS

Priority
|prī'ôrətē|
noun (pl. priorities)
a thing that is regarded as more important than another.

Introduction

Priority

"The art of the wise is knowing what to overlook . . ."

—William Blake

I know you recognize the following story. The names and situation may be different, but the story is the same, for it plays out all the time inside of companies around the globe:

Scene: A conference room inside a company's office with managers sitting around an oval conference table.

Issue: Deciding on a future strategic direction and customer base.

Manager 1:   We have a great offering that would fit perfectly with segment X, where market growth rates are off the charts.

Manager 2:   No, we need to go after market Y; the margins with this group are incredible.

Manager 3:   You're both wrong! We can't alienate our core. The largest market by far is Z, so our focus should be here.

Manager 4:   Our budget allocation for next year is constrained; how are we even going to fund this expansion? Perhaps we need to think about reorganizing.

We've all lived these conversations. Who usually wins? The person who wins is typically the one with the highest position on the org chart, the one who controls the budget, or who talks the loudest. But who *should* win? The one who's right.

Today more than ever, companies need to make choices about allocating scarce resources. Not only must they decide in what part of the market they should compete, but they must also adopt the right tactics for the part of the market in which they are competing. Moreover, just as important is the need to determine where *not* to compete. Doing precisely this—setting the right priorities at every stage of the process, from the 30,000-foot view of strategic vision to the detailed "in the weeds" tactics on the ground—is what good companies do at every step. How to set priorities at every decision point is what this book is about.

To illustrate, think for a moment about the obsolescence of mobile phones. That is: what if we didn't need phones anymore? We wouldn't have to worry about losing them, where they are, or if they'll ring at some inopportune time—because we'd be *wearing* them. Google's Project Glass aims to do just this. Google has developed glasses (really just one lens and hence the singular Project *Glass*)—which, at some point in the not-so-distant future, could easily morph into contact lenses or an item of clothing—that provide a heads-up display with all kinds of information projected onto the glass. They'll give users a weather forecast for the day, provide the optimal route for getting to your destination, keep your calendar appointments, video conference you into the person calling you, or broadcast what you are seeing to others (www.youtube.com/watch?v=9c6W4CCU9M4).

So, what do you think about the ability to wear your phone—one that can inform you every step of your day, from where to eat to a storm brewing later in the day (don't forget the umbrella) to the subway line being delayed or traffic on the highway? This isn't science fiction; it's reality, complete with a working prototype and planned market launch in 2014 (www.google.com/glass/start).

However, there is one thing in particular that Google Glass needs in order for it to succeed. It requires a seamless, always on, ultra-high-speed broadband wireless Internet connection. It must work in your home, out on the street, in the store, on a rooftop—all without disruption as you move from one wireless source to the next. Enter "Google Fiber." Google has launched a project (called Google Fiber, see https://fiber.google.com/about) in Kansas City to test the market for this, delivering ubiquitous ultra-high-speed broadband, both wired and wireless, throughout the city of Kansas City. It has begun rolling this out in various other locations in the United States (e.g., Provo, UT and Austin, TX), prompting headlines like "Google as Your ISP?" It's also starting to provide free Internet access in New York. There's a plan here, and it's brilliant.

Imagine that Google is able to establish this initiative throughout the United States. This would give it ownership of the key point of high-speed Internet access in this future market. It would essentially control the next-generation communication device beyond the smartphone. In this Google Glass environment, your Internet connection is paramount. If Google can develop and run the ubiquitous, omnipresent, ultra-high-speed broadband service, this—combined with the suite of services and products it already has in place—would make it virtually impossible for other players that own only one piece of the puzzle (such as Time Warner Cable, Comcast, or even Apple) to compete. The key to Google Glass and the next generation of communication and information devices is the ability to *own* the Internet connection.

Key Takeaway: What is Google's real priority here? Its goal is to own the Internet connection since owning this provides leverage for Google at every other point throughout what we will refer to later as the value chain and gives the company a complete solution that no one else can offer.

Now, imagine it's 2015 and Google has launched its high-speed Internet service throughout the United States. Imagine that you're a manager at Time Warner Cable or Comcast trying to sell Internet service or cable TV—both of which stop working when your customers walk out the door. I don't care how hard you work, how good you are at your job, or how many hours you put in; you simply can't compete against the ubiquitous, seamless Internet connection and Google Glass combination. Hence, there is only one battle that matters above all else for Google, Apple, Time Warner Cable, and all other content providers: the battle for the control of the Internet connection.

Figure I.1 illustrates the kind of content covered by key players Google, Apple, Amazon, Microsoft and Facebook. Note that only Google has complete coverage across the entire space—from Internet to Internet-enabled devices to a full set of applications. This allows it to leverage strengths in one market for advantage in another. Once Google is able to provide ubiquitous Wi-Fi, it can use Google Glass's strength—and all of its devices and applications—in a way that no other company can match.

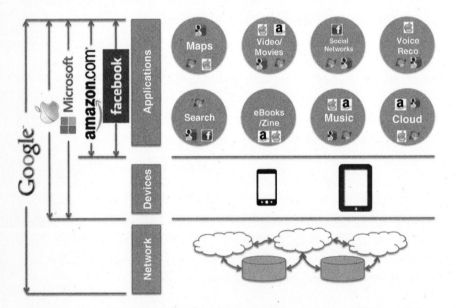

Figure I.1   Google is the only true end-to-end provider in the Internet space.

Key Takeaway: Google has mastered today's interconnected market environment like no other company has. It recognizes that the apps, the content, and the programs won't matter if someone else controls the connection. But when combined with what we will refer to later as a "Strategic Control Point"—in this case, the ubiquitous seamless Internet connection—Google Glass apps and operating system combine in a way that few, if any, can match.

General lesson for other businesses: Discovering and mastering a similar point of strategic control must be a central priority, because it is the key to success in today's environment.

By contrast, Nokia has seen significant declines in many major markets—largely because the company considered itself to be in the handset business. By the time it realized that it wasn't—that it was instead in the information and convenience business—the smartphone revolution had left the company in the dust. Ironically, Nokia actually had developed smartphone technology well ahead of the competition. However, it decided not to take the technology to market and bet instead on the continued growth it was enjoying in the handset market.[1] Unfortunately, growth can be a dangerous drug in the world of business—one that makes it easy to miss all of the warning signs. Good companies like Google are relentlessly looking to displace current growth with *new* avenues. And finding the *right* ways to grow is what this book is all about.

This book looks at when, where, why, and how you compete in one market space rather than another—and how you should set priorities at every step of the process. This applies to the big-vision issues previously mentioned all the way down to detailed tactics targeted at individual customers. From the C-suite to those on the front lines interacting with customers, this book focuses on those priorities that matter in a world that is changing faster than ever before.

It is all about priority.

Unfortunately, most companies lack a unified and integrated approach for addressing market opportunities. Very few have a rigorous set of tools and processes in place that enable them to recognize, prioritize, and set appropriate strategies in a way that maximizes shareholder value. Worse yet, different silos throughout the organization often have different processes in place. It is amazing how many companies—and how many people—I see working effectively in the market space in which they've been operating—without realizing that all of their work is fruitless. No matter how many hours they put in or how well they compete, they're doing it in vain if they are competing in the *wrong* space—in the part of the market that has low margins or where someone else can squeeze their margins through the ownership of what we will call "strategic control points." Thinking strategically about markets—and then forming a consistent, logical, and opportunistic approach—is a theme that we will revisit throughout this book. If your competitor has a better formulated and executed strategy, simply working hard won't do the trick.

On the Universal Nature of B2B Markets

There are a number of good books out there on how to win in strategy, and virtually all of them focus on what happens in *consumer markets*. While many of these cases are important, they don't matter if someone else owns a key ingredient, or if a competitor has locked distribution and shelf space access. These days, such intense focus on the consumer misses well over half the picture. A former colleague, Dr. Martin Koschat, once observed, "Nowadays, the *only* true consumer marketers are retailers . . . because they have the transactional relationship with the consumer. But even retailers—as customers of wholesalers and manufacturers—are players in B2B markets." The lesson: today, *every company* is a player in business-to-business (B2B) markets.[2]

. His point is well taken. Every company, even those operating in the consumer space, competes—and often derives its core competitive advantages—in the B2B space. Consider the biggest retailer imaginable: Walmart. Despite selling products to consumers, the store gains much of its strategic advantage in the market through supply chain and procurement efficiencies. And while much of Apple's success has been (appropriately) attributed to outstanding product design, its core engineering and ownership of the entire Apple ecosystem back to front (as we will see later) is at the center of its success.

Thus, both business-to-business and consumer examples are included throughout this book because we all can learn from the recent strategic moves of Amazon, Apple, Walmart, and others.

Consequently, this book is written based on two fundamental principles:

1. Today's business environment is radically and fundamentally different. We are experiencing fundamental change, the speed and magnitude of which is impacting business today in ways we've never seen before—ways that provide a once-in-a-lifetime opportunity. The role of information and the Internet— ubiquitous, always on, always interconnected—has permanently altered how firms compete and win. Just to drive home this point, consider the following examples that are discussed in chapters that follow:

   • Just four years ago, RIM (now BlackBerry) had a higher market share of the smartphone market than Apple and Samsung combined. Today, its market share is less than 5 percent.[3] Never before have we seen such rapid change.

   • Real estate commissions in the United States stood at 6 percent for more than a century, surviving U.S. Supreme Court rulings and Department of Justice lawsuits—that is, until the Multiple Listing Service (MLS) opened up to the Internet. Now, companies like Redfin have dramatically changed the structure of the brokerage industry and are rebating a portion of what has now become a 5 percent commission back to buyers. A standard business model and commission rate that has stood for almost a century has now begun to unravel after information (via MLS, which we refer to later as a "strategic control point") became accessible to anyone with a computer.

2. Effective strategy today requires a process that reflects appropriate priorities (referred to below as the "5/5 plan"). This changing world desperately needs a strategic process that reflects the appropriate priorities for today's business environment. Good companies prioritize at every step. The markets in which you compete, the part of the value chain upon which you focus, the set of customers you target, the alignment of tactics that support that strategy, and the allocation of resources to support it are all decisions you need to make with the *right priorities* in mind. And a process is necessary in order to ensure that you are doing this correctly. This book lays out, in detail, a five-point approach to appropriate strategic prioritization, combined with a five-point method for attracting high-priority customers (hence the "5/5 plan"). Good companies have a single-minded obsession with following the money. This book lays out a process that will naturally lead to success in the market.

Companies that succeed today—think Amazon or Google—do so because they recognize and use today's unique environment to their advantage. This book takes a cue from these organizations: how to compete in the *right space* in today's business environment. And any company can do this by following the proven, field-tested, logical process to strategy laid out here—one that begins with the decision to compete in the most attractive part of the market, focusing with the right priorities on the right customers, and using tactics that resonate and deliver to those customers. The logical process begins at the 30,000-foot level and sequentially narrows down the field of view, ending up with the tactics that help deliver the 30,000-foot vision with focus. Specifically, the key steps in sequence are illustrated in Figure I.2.

Like any pyramid, the base is important. Build any layer on top of a weak base and it is a recipe for disaster. If external trends are going against you, it won't matter how well you do on items two through five (just ask Kodak). Compete in the wrong part of the value chain

Figure I.2 A 5-point approach to compete in the right space with the right strategic priorities.

and get squeezed by someone who owns a better position, and your segmentation and tactics won't matter (just ask Borders, which lost out to Amazon.com and others); do a great job with items one through three and choose the wrong segments, you will not do as well as a competitor that goes after the right segments. You get the point. You must build each part of the pyramid's five-step process of prioritization on a solid foundation—and reinforce what is below. Consequently, the chapters in this book are laid out in the same logical order, with each step building on a solid foundation:

1. External business environment and overall market assessment
   - Assessing the core and growth opportunities via adjacent markets
2. Value chain, strategic control points, and capabilities assessment
3. Segmentation analysis and development—pivot to tactics and the importance of understanding customer needs through choice analysis
4. "Incentive alignment"—vertical strategic alignment and asset specificity

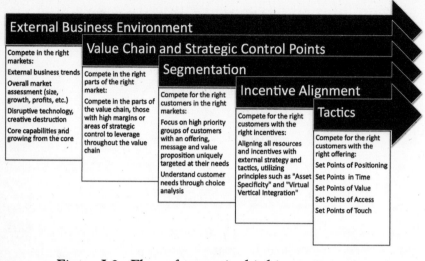

External Business Environment

Compete in the right markets:

External business trends

Overall market assessment (size, growth, profits, etc.)

Disruptive technology, creative destruction

Core capabilities and growing from the core

Value Chain and Strategic Control Points

Compete in the right parts of the right market:

Compete in the parts of the value chain, those with high margins or areas of strategic control to leverage throughout the value chain

Segmentation

Compete for the right customers in the right markets:

Focus on high priority groups of customers with an offering, message and value proposition uniquely targeted at their needs

Understand customer needs through choice analysis

Incentive Alignment

Compete for the right customers with the right incentives:

Aligning all resources and incentives with external strategy and tactics, utilizing principles such as "Asset Specificity" and "Virtual Vertical Integration"

Tactics

Compete for the right customers with the right offering:

Set Points of Positioning

Set Points in Time

Set Points of Value

Set Points of Access

Set Points of Touch

Figure I.3   Flow of strategic thinking to compete in the right space.

5. Setting tactics—five points:

- Points of Positioning: unique and winning value propositions
- Points in Time: offering timing
- Points of Value: principles in extracting value
- Points of Access: points of customer access
- Points of Touch: customer touch as the embodiment of your strategy

We start at a broad, high level and narrow the lens through which we view the market opportunity further with each step. Figure I.3 illustrates both the flow of the chapters in this book and the process a company should follow.

Decision Timeline

The goal of this process is to make conscious decisions about where to compete, each decision made with the right priorities. As noted previously, you can compete well—but if you're competing in the wrong part of the market—in areas where margins are thin or where others can squeeze them—you will lose in the long run. Compete in the right markets with the right priorities, and success will come much more easily than if you were simply working *harder*.

The various concepts and methodologies we'll discuss in this book that can be applied directly to your own particular situation are as follows:

- External business environment and market assessment
- Core versus adjacent market analysis
- Value chain analysis and the use of strategic control points
- Competitive capability assessment and capability gap analysis
- Segmentation analysis and strategic prioritization
- Choice analysis applied at both the individual and in aggregate
- Horizontal and vertical incentive alignment and asset specificity
- The five points of effective tactics:
  - Points of Positioning
  - Points in Time
  - Points of Value
  - Points of Access
  - Points of Touch

Implementing such radically different approaches and ways of thinking about markets, competitors, and customers may require a fundamental shift in your company's culture. Many have claimed that changing an organization's corporate culture would inherently initiate the change needed to generate breakthrough strategy—that is, change the culture and success will naturally follow.

The concepts laid out in this book suggest something fundamentally different. Culture follows the money and success. Change the incentive structure and all else will follow—from internal stakeholders to the organization's corporate governance to external stakeholders. It has been the hallmark of successful companies—from IBM to Nike to Apple to Amazon to Google and of successful leaders such as Steve Jobs and Jeff Bezos—to live the concept that change follows money. This is a central theme of this book.

It is important to note that many of the concepts, tools, and methodologies that we'll cover have only been developed in the academic literature over the last 10 years or so. Therefore, they've only been integrated in piecemeal fashion in the business press over the last few years. Hence, this book provides the insight, tools, methodologies, and strategic thinking to enable firms to uniquely compete with strategic advantage in today's market environment.

This book's objective is to provide a useful, functional examination of the opportunities for those operating in today's business environment. Each chapter begins with a story that illustrates the key issue that chapter will address. In order to highlight the lessons learned, each chapter will end with two lists of the most important items discussed throughout: a Chapter Summary and Key Business Principles and Key Business Tools.

Today's business environment is perhaps the most exciting, dynamic, and rapidly evolving in history. The impact of technology on not only our personal lives but on every single thing we do in business, large or small, gives us a once-in-a-lifetime—perhaps once-in-many-generations—opportunity to make a lasting impact on the future business landscape. We need practical, state-of-the-art tools and processes to make this happen—hence, the motivation for writing this book in the first place. Use the book to your advantage—and success.

> *I don't want to be just one step ahead of the competition; I want to be so far ahead that they can't find me.*
> —Michael J. Cave, CEO, Boeing Capital

CHAPTER 1

The Importance of Fundamentals

"Rizzutoisms" in practice and why structure matters: Thinking "out of the box" without having a box in the first place can be dangerous.

—Phil Rizzuto and "Rizzutoisms"

B efore we can "think out of the box," it is important to have a box in the first place. Attempting to attack a business problem in a new or inventive way without having a solid foundation in place first can be dangerous. To illustrate what happens to companies that fail to start with fundamentals, we begin this chapter with the story of Phil Rizzuto.

Phil Rizzuto, known in the baseball world as "The Scooter," was an interesting character. A former shortstop for the New York Yankees and 1954 American League Most Valuable Player, he is enshrined in the Baseball Hall of Fame in Cooperstown, NY. He is perhaps better known as their longtime television announcer (some of you might remember him as the former spokesperson for *The Money Store* or for his being featured in the Meatloaf song "Paradise by the Dashboard Light"). However, he is probably best known for his colorful and convoluted comments.

To illustrate, Phil Rizzuto and his coannouncer, Bobby Murcer, were announcing a game between the New York Yankees and the Milwaukee Brewers. It was a slow Sunday afternoon game, and the two announcers were just trying to kill dead airtime. Now, for non-baseball fans, there are only two things that you need to know about baseball in order for this story to make sense: (1) every game has a winner and a loser—if the game is tied at the end of regulation (nine innings), the two teams go into overtime (extra innings) until one team wins; and (2) games are played during the day and at night. Other than these two facts, you need not know anything about baseball in order for this story to make sense. In any event, here is how Bob Frank, an economist at Cornell University at the time, tells the story:[1]

The cable TV system where I live in Ithaca, New York, carries most New York Yankee baseball games. One August night, sportscasters

Phil Rizzuto and Bobby Murcer were calling a slow game between the Yankees and the Milwaukee Brewers. Between pitches, Rizzuto was looking over his record sheets and remarked that the Brewers had done much better in day games than in [night] games. Murcer checked his own records and found that the Yankees, too, had a much higher winning percentage during the day. With characteristic enthusiasm, Rizzuto then conjectured that all teams have better records for day games. In a brisk exchange of the sort that makes summer evenings in Ithaca seem to fly by, the two then spent the rest of the inning discussing the poor lighting conditions in American League parks and various other difficulties that might help account for why teams do so poorly at night.

But the "fact" that Rizzuto and Murcer were trying to explain was of course not a fact at all. Without consulting any baseball records, we know that it is mathematically impossible for all teams to have better records during the day than at night. For every team that loses a night game, some other team must win one. Lighting conditions at night may indeed be poor, but they are poor for both sides. Taken as a whole, teams play .500 ball at night, the same as they do during the day.

What is wrong with this picture? As Bob Frank explains: it is simply not possible for *all* teams to have better records during day games *or* during night games. If every game has a winner and a loser, teams win an average of 50 percent of their games during the day and 50 percent of their games at night. This is an example of the convoluted logic that pervades business thinking today—and what we will refer to as a "Rizzutoism" throughout the book.[2]

Unfortunately, such convoluted logic isn't isolated to baseball game announcers; it abounds in business as well. Examples are almost endless and they range from the silly to the sublime to the serious. Australian telecom provider Optus once had a tagline: "We make you feel like you're the only one in the world with a telephone." Think about that for a moment. Perdue Chicken's slogan, "It takes a tough man to make a tender chicken," was translated into Spanish as, "It takes a particularly virile man to impregnate an affectionate chicken"—leading customers to wonder exactly what Perdue was selling.

Rizzutoisms in business aren't limited to silly taglines—substantive examples abound. Cost-plus pricing, product-based segmentation, and distributional asymmetric incentive structures are all serious examples that we'll discuss later. For now, however, we will use the term Rizzutoism to refer to the use of convoluted logic in business.

A concrete business example of a Rizzutoism in practice is that of R.J. Reynolds Tobacco Co.'s introduction of Premier cigarettes in the late 1980s—an example made famous in the book *Barbarians at the Gate*.[3] R.J. Reynolds Tobacco had developed the first "smokeless cigarette," an interesting technological innovation. On one tip of the cigarette was a piece of carbon placed in front of the tobacco, while the inside of the cigarette consisted of a piece of aluminum with the tobacco wrapped around it. The filter on the other end also had a piece of carbon in the middle of it. When the cigarette was ignited by a lighter, the carbon essentially "lit" the cigarette from the inside so that it produced virtually no secondhand smoke. The only smoke in the room was that which had already been filtered by the smoker's lungs (i.e., upon exhale)!

In principle, this was a great idea: it attempted to allay peoples' fear of secondhand smoke, providing a new product push into a staid and declining business. R.J. Reynolds made a $350 million investment that, at first glance, was a reasonable business move. However, problems began to emerge as the test market results came in—and weren't that impressive. Less than 5 percent of respondents said that they would try the product again. In fact, the most common terms used to describe the product was that it tasted like "shit" (literally, the word that was used) and it smelled like a "fart." The problem was that the cigarette tasted horrible and when the carbon tip was lit by a match, rather than the requisite lighter, the sulfur reacted with the carbon to give off a fart smell. Not exactly what you want to use to describe your product—as James Garner's (playing Ross Johnson, the CEO of R.J. Reynolds at the time) line in the movie by the same name said, "Tastes like shit and smells like a fart; that's one unique advertising slogan." When introduced in the market, the product's repeat rates—so crucial to its success—were less than 1 percent.

Now, all of this isn't the Rizzutoism; attempting to innovate and introduce a smokeless cigarette had the potential for success. The Rizzutoism occurred *after* Reynolds spent $350 million developing this product and after it found out that it tasted like $#!+ and smelled like a #@&+. At that point, the company spent an additional $350 million *launching* the dang thing! Note that "sunk costs" should be irrelevant in this case: having already lost $350 million on developing the product isn't a good reason to lose *another* $350 million. We could argue as to why they decided to proceed with the launch after the poor test results: *Barbarians at the Gate* provides an excellent account—arrogance, the sunk-cost fallacy, leveraged buyout motives, to name a few. But regardless of the motives, losing nearly three-quarters of a billion dollars on a product that was an abysmal failure in the market could have been avoided early on. The decision to do the research and develop the product was not the Rizzutoism; the decision to *launch* it after knowing the customer reaction was!

Sunk Cost Fallacy

Sunk costs should be irrelevant to future decisions. Yet we all make these mistakes in various decisions in our lives—in both the professional and personal realms. Be honest—have you ever held onto a stock arguing that "I can't sell it now; I've lost so much already"? Your real decision should be making the best investment with the money you have left. In business, executives can become emotionally involved with the projects in which they invest. Not all these projects are good investments. To avoid deeper losses, it is important to adopt a periodic review process where reviewers are not invested (professionally or emotionally) executives. These reviews (often referred to as non-advocacy reviews) should occur at each key stage of product development (with the option of termination), and again post-launch (if it gets that far). Thus, a non-performing project can be identified early on, and the company may avoid deep financial losses by overcoming the sunk-cost fallacy that leads to escalation bias—throwing good money after bad at a bad investment.

Distinguishing Rizzutoisms and Sheer Folly from Business Brilliance

Distinguishing a Rizzutoism and sheer folly from ingenious insight and business brilliance can sometimes be a fine line. To illustrate: imagine it was 40 years ago and I put the following proposition on the desk of your venture capital (VC) firm. I've presented you with a business plan and a request for $50 million.

> We propose to build a series of retail establishments beginning in one region of the country and eventually expanding throughout the United States and then internationally. We will do no advertising. Our stores will become so ubiquitous that, in some cities, we will position our stores on each corner of various four-corner intersections. We will provide couches and amenities so that customers can just sit in our stores all day for free. And, we will sell only one thing: $3 cups of coffee. Invest in my company?

This is, of course, a simplistic representation of Howard Schulz's vision for what was to become the behemoth that we know as Starbucks.

The average cup of coffee in the late 1980s when he started to build Starbucks cost $0.70. It was sold through a deli or convenience store, and its taste often caused people to refer to it as "swill." Customers were clamoring for better coffee. However, customers were not clamoring to pay *more* for a cup of coffee, which was fine— because Howard Schulz wasn't selling coffee. His genius was making a connection to the coffee culture in Europe by recognizing the *latent* attributes, the things *besides* coffee that customers were willing to pay for. These, of course, included ambience, image, a reward for a hard day's work (most of us can afford a $3 cup of coffee, after all), and a "third place" (that is, a place to go besides home and the office— other than a bar). Howard Schulz recognized that people would be willing to pay for this third place. While San Francisco-based chain Peet's Coffee was taking the seats out of its retail establishments in order to deter homeless men and women from lounging in its stores, Starbucks was making its couches and chairs more comfortable to *encourage* the coffee culture that it was promoting.[4] And the rest, as they say, is history.

The Key Is Attributes, Not Core Competencies

A crucial difference between Reynolds's Rizzutoism and Howard Schulz's brilliance is the latter's understanding of the customer's willingness to pay for attributes. We discuss the use of choice analysis[5] to assess and quantify preferences in detail in Chapter 6. For now, we begin with some intuition and an example.[6]

The following simple example drives home the importance of focusing on attribute-based decision making rather than core competencies. Although it's a business-to-consumer example, the principles apply even more strongly in a business-to-business (B2B) environment.

To illustrate, imagine you are in the market for a color printer. Get out a piece of paper and a pen or pencil and write down all of the reasons and qualities that would make you choose one printer over another. Presumably, your list would include things like print resolution, print speed, the cost of the printer and "consumables" such as ink and toner cartridges, the ability to scan or fax, and so on. Now imagine you are in the market for a new automobile and write down the reasons why you would buy one automobile versus another. This list would likely include things like miles per gallon, body type, brand, price, safety ratings, repair costs, image, and so on.

These are all attributes of the offering at hand—the things that matter when we buy a product, be it at home or at work. Where in the world on these lists of attributes that you have created are the *core competencies*[7] (capabilities) of Hewlett-Packard or General Motors? Nowhere. And this is because we decide what to buy based on the offering's underlying *attributes*—not on the basis of the company's capabilities or core competencies. Yet time and time again, companies attempt to compete on the basis of their core competencies.

It's not that core competencies aren't important; to the contrary, they are what enable a company to produce the attributes that customers seek out and value. However, the focus should be outward in, rather than inward out. A company must first concentrate on the qualities or amenities that customers value and then develop core competencies that deliver these key attributes—specifically, in a way that provides a competitive advantage on the key salient differentiators. Many companies in the B2B space focus on what they do well rather than focus on what customers want. It is a critical distinction.

A few years back, British Airways conducted an "intercept" survey of business travelers departing London's Heathrow Airport. After screening to ensure that the respondent was traveling on business, surveyors asked travelers to imagine that they were flying from Heathrow to New York's John F. Kennedy Airport. The surveyors had the respondents name the top three reasons why they would choose one airline over another. Think about what your top three would be. In the British Airway's survey, the Heathrow travelers named the following three: (1) safety, (2) route, and (3) schedule.

Let's think about this a bit, one at a time. Which is the safest airline? Though we can't say for sure which one is, we can probably eliminate some. Would you want to fly on Aeroflot on a Yak-42, for example? But aside from those that we eliminate, we can't really differentiate one major airline from another. So, let's examine the second most important attribute: route. I don't know about you, but if I were to fly from London to New York, I would kind of want to fly nonstop; I guess there's always the Icelandair flight that stops in Reykjavik. However, again, in terms of route, I can't differentiate one major carrier from another. What about schedule? Flights are so tightly packed on that route that there are usually seven or eight flights to choose from. So then how do I make my decision?

Enter salient differentiators.

While safety, route, and schedule may be the most important attributes, when all major competitors are equal on these key attributes (as is often the case), consumers typically make their actual decisions based on what we refer to as "salient differentiators." In this case, these would be things like frequent flyer miles, flat beds in business class, on-time performance, and so on. The first three—safety, route, and schedule—are places where you can lose business. However, since they generally aren't points of differentiation in this market, they're not places where you can *win* business. It's certainly necessary to do these successfully; however, it's not sufficient. The firms that focus on the must-haves (here, safety, route and schedule) and end up on par with rivals ultimately lose business—particularly if their rivals focus on the areas that drive customers' purchase decisions, the "salient differentiators." Thus, you won't gain share by highlighting your airline's safety, since all airlines are equally safe. However, emphasizing your superior on-time performance or business class may indeed attract customers from your rivals. Make sure you have the "must haves" right, but recognize that it's the "salient differentiators" that often win or lose the business.

Note that, occasionally, you can turn the must-haves into salient differentiators. Boeing's 787 Dreamliner, for example, has turned route into a differentiator for both Boeing and its customers. The new, fuel-efficient plane can travel longer-haul point-to-point routes using 20 percent less fuel than traditional aircraft. Hence, airlines may be able to profitably fly routes nonstop that required going through a hub before. This has the potential to create a huge strategic advantage for both the Boeing Company and the airlines that fly the 787—wouldn't you prefer a nonstop flight to one that requires a stop and a change of planes?

Think how important these elements are in your own purchase decisions—convenience with respect to mobile phones, for example. Think about it: is there another product for which we would accept such poor quality—dropped calls, not enough coverage, all those extra fees—as we get from our current mobile phones? Can you imagine getting in your car and having it turn off mid-trip, forcing you to start it again over and over? Or hitting the accelerator knowing that it will only respond some of the time?

So why do we accept such poor call quality in mobile phones? *Convenience.* We gladly trade off—and pay dearly for—the convenience of getting and making a call or using data, at any place, at any time (well, almost). Do we like dealing with these issues? Of course we don't. Would we prefer the call quality of a landline? Of course we would. But, we pay for convenience. All attributes aren't created equal.

Business Question: What are the must-haves in your markets—the equivalent of safety, route, and schedule in the British Airways example? What are the table stakes on which you need to compete, but that won't win the customer's business? And what are the salient differentiators, those that will ultimately win the business?

The Master of Salient Differentiators: Apple

Question: What do all of the products below have in common?

1. Motorola ROKR
2. Pippin
3. eWorld
4. Taligent
5. Cyberdog
6. Macintosh TV
7. Macintosh Portable
8. 20th Anniversary Mac
9. Lisa
10. Newton

Answer: They were all made by Apple—that invincible Cupertino, California, machine—and they were all *failures*.

These failures are even more startling to consider when you think of the journey the company has taken in less than 10 years' time. Back in 2006, Apple was the darling of the tech world for its transformation from Apple Computer Inc. to a company known for iTunes and iPods—often cited as the brand to emulate when transforming a company to new market opportunities. However, leader Steve Jobs's brilliance came from his refusal to ever rest—his need to always move forward ahead of market trends. While Apple could easily have continued to build on its success in digital music, proliferating its iPod lineup and distribution, Jobs knew that the market was evolving. Hence, Apple decided to lead the market trend rather than defend its existing market. In mid-2007, while iPods were still selling like hotcakes, Apple released the iPhone—the iPod that is also a phone. Though it was offered at a significantly higher price point, the demand for iPhones skyrocketed. The iPhone cannibalized the demand for iPods—who needs an iPod when we have one in our phone? But, to

Apple, this was just fine since it was ceding sales of lower margin iPods to higher margin iPhones (and eventually iPads). This was creative destruction at its best.

Lesson: Cannibalize your own products or someone else will.

Fast forward to 2013. By this time, over 70 percent of Apple's revenue came from the iPhone and the iPad—products that hadn't even existed five years earlier. It is an excellent and startling example of how successful companies never stop innovating, while other companies spend all their time defending existing turf and, consequently, let the world pass them by (see Figure 1.1).

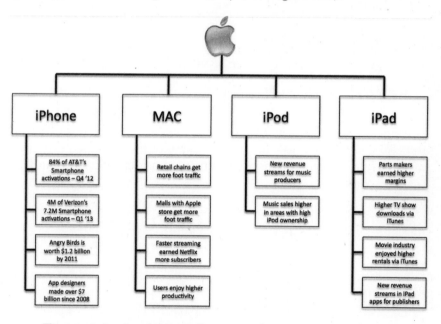

Figure 1.1   Apple's product transformation—Creative destruction at its best.

Source: "84% of AT&T's Smartphone activations - Q4'12" (AT&T Q4 2012 quarterly earning's report); "4M of Verizon's 7.2M Smartphone activations—Q1'13" (Verizon Q1 2013 quarterly earning's report); Angry Birds is worth $1.2 billion by 2011 (www.mashable.com), 2011/08/12; "App designer made over $7 billion since 2008" (Apple press Jan. 7, 2013). Remainder of chart: conversation with various experts and industry observations.

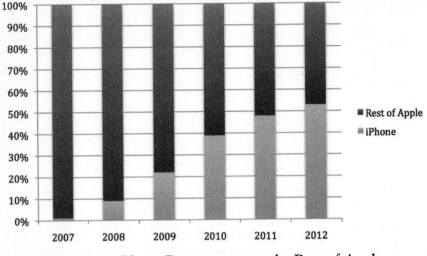

Figure 1.2   iPhone Revenue versus the Rest of Apple.

Apple has come a long way from the Newton—perhaps its biggest failure—to the iPhone—its biggest success—something that is easy to see in Figure 1.2. When the iPhone was introduced in 2007, the revenue it generated was negligible compared to that of the rest of the company. Less than five years later, it accounts for more than half the revenue of the entire company—more than quadrupling from 2007 to 2012. This happened on top of Apple's already impressive annual revenue growth over the previous five years, and the reason for it is simple: the company was in the right place at the right time. The iPhone wasn't even remotely the first smartphone; there were already a number of smartphones in the market when Apple entered. Nokia and Erickson had pioneered the category, and, as a result, the mobile phone data network was relatively mature, which meant that the underlying infrastructure was there to support the product. Had the iPhone entered the market when the only available option for mobile data was AT&T's relatively slow Edge technology, it would have never achieved the success it did.

Accordingly, the logic of strategic decisions ideally follows a process[8]—a process that is outlined next and throughout the book. It begins with an understanding of the external business environment—

those things that we can't control. These macro trends often define the future of disruptive technologies in an industry. No one wants to be the metaphorical equivalent of a $5\frac{1}{4}$-inch floppy drive manufacturer today. Once this broad, big-picture understanding of the market's future direction is clear, you can move on to analyzing the industry "value chain." Until we address this in more detail later, you can think of this process as a flow from raw material all the way through to delivering an offering to a customer—including providing post-sales support once you've delivered it.

The next step is to establish key strategic control points to ensure that you are competing in the right parts of the market. There are countless examples of companies that make all the right strategic moves, hire all the right people, but still do not do well as an organization simply because they are competing in the wrong part of the market—one where the margins are low or strategic leverage or scale economies are not possible.

Once an organization has defined the appropriate part of the market and assessed the broad trends and disruptive technologies affecting its industry, it should have a good sense of where to compete. The next step is to prioritize its focus within that part of the market utilizing segmentation analysis. If conducted properly, a segmentation analysis should be all about focus and prioritization. Hence, segmentation requires companies to focus on priorities and positioning. Only *after* the firm has done this well can it begin to determine its tactics— elements like price, positioning, route to market and points of access, communications and points of touch, and entry strategy. You can only begin to consider broader components such as brand, detailed positioning, organizational structure, customer contact plans, and so on, once this process's outcomes are clear.

Process

As noted previously, the phrase "thinking outside of the box"— popular as it may be—can be dangerous without having a box to provide structure in the first place. This isn't unique to B2C markets; given their complexity, the logic of strategic process becomes all the more important in B2B markets. Good strategic decisions are made based on logic and process. A process doesn't have to stifle creativity. However, it should alert you when the creative process has diverted from the business objective and help focus your efforts on what matters to your objectives. Remember: good companies have a single-minded obsession with following the money.

As noted in the introduction, this book follows a rigorous, proven[9] five-step process of strategic development. Think of this as a process for the treatment of "Random Strategy Disorder" (RSD), a leading cause of business Rizzutoisms today. In detail, the book will follow this process in the following order:

1. External Business Environment, Market Assessment, Growth Opportunities
   a. Understand and evaluate the external market environment—assess and understand all of those things that we don't control—examine macro trends, disruptive technologies, and so on.
   b. Conduct a detailed market assessment—systematically assess the attractiveness of addressable market opportunities—before you compete in a market space, be sure it's attractive enough to invest in.
   c. Thoroughly evaluate core versus adjacent markets—the objective should be to grow from the core to adjacent markets without straying too far from the core.
2. Value Chain and Strategic Control Points
   a. Map out the relevant value chain(s)—competing in the right space starts with following the money in order to compete in the parts of the value chain that command the highest margins, generate the most cash flow, enable you to leverage competitively horizontally and vertically, and so on.

b. Assess strategic control points within the value chain—this is the key to strategy overall, something that companies such as Apple, Google and Amazon have incorporated into their processes.

c. Understand customer needs and competency gaps and advantages throughout the value chain on both the B2B and B2C side—employ techniques such as customer choice analysis, competitive capability assessment and capability gap analysis.

3. Segment based on Customer Needs—the Pivot to Tactics

a. Strategically prioritize segments and follow the money with rigid discipline.

b. Create value propositions by segment.

4. Align Incentives

a. Align across all internal and external constituents.

b. Use the concept of "asset specificity."

c. Utilize concept of "virtual vertical integration" where possible.

5. Set Tactics—Five Points of Tactics

a. Points of Positioning: unique and winning value propositions.

b. Points in Time: offering and entry timing.

c. Points of Value: principles in extracting value.

d. Points of Access: points of customer access.

e. Points of Touch: customer touch as the embodiment of your strategy.

This book's outline and chapters follow the strategic process flow above. First, understand the market. Second, assess the market opportunities. Third, find the opportunity space where margins, profit, and growth are available and where you have competencies that provide a sustainable competitive advantage. Fourth, segment the market properly so that you have the correct priorities. Employ the Willie Sutton rule of following the money by using targeted deployment tactics that match your priorities.[10] Fifth, develop tactics that account for vertical/horizontal and internal/external incentive alignment, utilizing strategic game theory principles. Additionally, use customer discovery tools such as choice and conjoint analysis. Finally, integrate your plan throughout the organization and across internal and external stakeholders. Integrate, prioritize and align; it's what good companies do.

The Importance of Reinforcing Business Models

All aspects of the process detailed above must be self-reinforcing. A high-service, low-price business model is generally not a good idea as the higher costs associated with delivering a high level of service usually require charging higher prices in order to be profitable. Business models build on each other; if even just one element is inconsistent with the rest of the model, achieving success will be difficult at best.

Consider the now-cliché cases of Southwest Airlines and Walmart—organizations that have successfully combined low-cost operations with low-priced market offerings. And there are many others that we will discuss throughout the book: Apple, Amazon, Redfin, and more. Perhaps two quick counter-examples will drive home the importance of lining up all aspects of the process.

Grocery Delivery

The business model for fast-moving consumer goods and grocery products is a high-volume low-margin one that is often cutthroat at the retail level. Home delivery in the United States is generally expensive to provide, given the distances between residences and the various costs associated with delivery. Hence, in any location other than a densely populated urban environment, the cost of delivery and the scale of operations needed are simply inconsistent with a low-margin business. As a result, grocery delivery has generally been unsuccessful and unprofitable in the United States.

Perhaps the most notorious of these failures was that of Webvan, a San Francisco Bay area delivery service that went bankrupt in 2001. By contrast, leading U.K. retailer Tesco successfully pioneered home delivery of its own products in London, at about the same time Webvan was failing. Of course, London is a densely populated city whose underlying delivery economics are more consistent with the low-margin grocery business. Further, Tesco initiated a launch backed by solid research: detailed consumer investigation indicated that Londoners were willing to pay five pounds sterling—no more—for a typical delivery. Given central London's density and Tesco's market share (about 30 percent), the company estimated that it could make deliveries at or below that five-pound limit. In the end, delivery would break even, but Tesco's market share would increase—as would profitability!

To summarize this discussion:[11]

Webvan (Silicon Valley, United States)	Tesco (London)
Low margins on grocery products	Low margins on grocery products
Large distances between houses	Short distances between flats
Long delivery time per delivery	Short delivery time per delivery
High fuel and delivery cost per delivery	Relatively low labor but high fuel costs
Delivery costs much higher relative to large-scale willingness to pay	Delivery costs in line with large-scale customer willingness to pay
Low relative volume of home delivery	30 percent share meant larger volumes
Delivery for multiple retailers, so no competitive advantage for any single retailer	Tesco-only delivery meant a competitive advantage by growing share for Tesco

Tesco's model reinforced itself: low margins for the products it distributed and relatively low costs for delivery that were commensurate with customer willingness to pay. As a result, the company was able to grow share in the London market. Webvan, by contrast, had a more expensive infrastructure and delivery costs without a significantly higher customer willingness to pay—at least not in sufficient volume to make the business profitable. Webvan eventually tried to offer value-added items in an attempt to recoup delivery costs, but again, there wasn't sufficient volume and willingness to pay to support this effort. Hence, there was an inherent disconnect in terms of higher costs inside of a low-margin business. Thus, unlike Tesco's model, Webvan's included a cost structure that led to its eventual failure.

What's the lesson here? Make sure to use the process in this book to develop a business model and offering that reinforces itself (Tesco) rather than one that contradicts itself (Webvan). Although much of this book won't focus on the reinforcing aspects of business models explicitly, every aspect of the book will utilize this principle implicitly in all that follows.

Chapter Summary and Key Business Principles

- In order to think outside the box, you must first have and understand the box in the first place. Appreciating the business fundamentals is the initial crucial step to sound strategy.

- Beware of Rizzutoisms—a phrase defined as "convoluted logic in business."

- Investing in innovation, but ending up with an unsuccessful product, isn't necessarily a Rizzutoism because even good companies fail from time to time. However, falling victim to the sunk-cost fallacy and launching product in the face of negative prelaunch evidence *is*.

- There is a fine line between Rizzutoism and business brilliance.

- Salient differentiators are what drive purchase decisions. Companies should develop/refocus core competencies that would provide competitive advantages on these elements of their offerings.

- Focus on attributes, not core competencies—develop core competencies to meet the needed attributes in the market.

- In order for a new product/service to launch successfully, companies must consider the timing of the entry, that is, supporting business infrastructure must be well in place.

- Business models should *reinforce*; all aspects of the business model must complement each other. You are only as good as your weakest element.

Key Business Tools

- Attribute-based analysis (focusing on salient differentiators in a way that can win the high-priority business).

- Analysis of external market environment, disruptive technologies, and creative destruction (examining external market forces, which are all of those things that we can't control), trends and understanding the market in a way that prioritizes creating new market opportunities.

- Market assessment (prioritizing markets based on opportunities available using objective metrics of market attractiveness).

- Strategic control points (areas of the market or value chain that, if owned or controlled, allow firms to extract greater margins and control other parts of the opportunity space).

- Value chain and capabilities map (tracing value creation throughout the scope of a firm's operations and mapping the key capabilities needed in these areas in detail).

Finding the Right Market Opportunities

External Business Environment and Overall Market Assessment
—The "Corner Restaurant Rizzutoism"

W eeki Wachee is a small, sleepy town on the west coast of Florida, best known for its mermaids. Yes, you read that right—mermaids. Weeki Wachee Springs State Park (www.weekiwachee.com), visited by celebrities from Elvis to Larry the Cable Guy, was founded in 1947 and has had continuous underwater mermaid shows ever since (see Figure 2.1).

Just down the road from Weeki Wachee State Park on Highway 19 was a local restaurant by the name of Sandy's. Sandy's served a great breakfast—eggs, hash browns, and the like—a fast lunch and a complete home-cooked dinner for $9.95. Despite its great service and food, Sandy's stayed in business for only 18 months before running out of cash. The volume of traffic on Highway 19 just couldn't support Sandy's expenses. The building was already outfitted with a kitchen and for table service, so the space didn't need to be refitted for the next tenants. Soon enough, another eatery—a more upscale place this time around—rented it fairly quickly. Because the new owners had migrated from New York, the fare was more extravagant, and the restaurant opened only for lunch and dinner. Unfortunately for the owners, the menu proved too expensive for the local community, which was composed of many retirees—and it folded after about 18 months as well. Once again, the restaurant-ready space rented quickly to a retired couple that opened another family restaurant serving breakfast, lunch, and dinner. This pair fared a bit better than the previous two, managing to stay in business for almost two full years before realizing that the cash and traffic flow just couldn't support the restaurant's expenses.

This chain of events continued on for another five failed restaurant ventures at the same location. Each new owner assumed that (1) the upfront expenses would be lower since the building was already outfitted with a kitchen and ready for table service; and (2) he or she had a better idea than the previous proprietors.

Figure 2.1   Weeki Wachee Springs State Park, Home of the Mermaid Show.

Enter business number nine. Yes, yet another restaurant at the same location. If you think this story will now go on about how and why restaurant number nine succeeded where the previous eight failed, you will be disappointed. While a story with a happy ending would have been nice, it also would have flown in the face of business logic.

Why in the world did restaurateur number nine think he would somehow succeed with essentially the same business in the same location where the previous eight had failed? There are several traps into which businesses often fall.

1. *Cost-driven decisions*. We often assume that if costs are lower, it may be a good deal—and sometimes it is. Certainly, all other things being equal, lower costs are better than higher costs. However, it's not the driving factor in this business. As in any real estate consideration, it's about location, location, location. Low costs won't help if you have an insufficient volume of traffic.

2. *Lack of attention to history.* One could argue that the owner of the second restaurant was the only smart one. After all, one failed restaurant does not constitute a pattern and the second owner did, indeed, have lower entry costs. But after that second restaurant failed, future restaurateurs should have gotten the message that this probably wasn't a great location for a restaurant.

3. *Arrogance.* Each new business owner likely believed that "we're different; we're better. *We* can make this work." Enough said.

4. *Hope.* "I hope" is not a strategy; nor is I think, I feel, I believe. Imagine being on a plane where the conversation between pilot and copilot is as follows:

   Pilot to copilot: "I *hope* you remembered to put down the landing gear."

   Copilot's response: "Well, I *think* I did."

   It wouldn't be very reassuring to be a passenger on this plane. And I'm not sure I'd be any more reassured to work for a business leader with a similar lack of conviction.[1]

5. *The "all in" decision.* The tragedy of this story is that these business owners were all retired people who invested much of their life savings in the business. They were hoping to attain their lifelong dream of running a restaurant. But again— hope is not a strategy. Use this book; heed the lessons of history. For as we know, those who fail to do so are doomed to repeat it!

The external business environment can be succinctly defined as *those things that we cannot control.* No matter how large or small our organization, we do not have power over factors like the aggregate growth rate, inflation, exchange rate, balance of trade, and so forth. There are two examples that illustrate this on a more micro level: Time Inc.'s Time Distribution Services (TDS) division and MP3.com.

TDS—A Transition to the Publishing Supply Chain of Today

Time, Inc. is the largest publisher of magazines in the United States, and counts publications such as *Time*, *Sports Illustrated*, and *People* in its stable of over 30 magazines. In 2011, the company accounted for 21 percent of the total U.S. consumer magazine advertising revenue. Over the past 20 years, it has had at least two main enemies. Today, of course, it's the Internet and e-publishing that's revolutionizing the industry; we'll expand on this in a minute. But *Time*'s first enemy is the growth of self-checkout units. As of the end of 2008, there were 92,600 self-checkout units worldwide. The number is estimated to reach 430,000 units by 2014.[2] Why is this a problem for magazine publishers? Take a look at the one shown in Figure 2.2.

Where do you put the magazines? And even if you could find a place to put them, the customer is too busy scanning and bagging to purchase one. It turns out that there is an optimal wait time to encourage shoppers to purchase magazines: if it's too short—or if they're too busy checking out—they never have the chance to purchase. If, on the other hand, customers wait too long, they may

Figure 2.2   A typical self-service checkout stand.

read the one article that would have compelled them to buy the magazine and put it back. None of this encourages magazine sales. Further, while the newsstand contributes 25 percent of non-advertising based revenue, it contributes 32 percent of net profit (overall, advertising contributes 64 percent of net revenue).[3]

A second major enemy of magazine publishers has been the consolidation of the retail environment. For example, most major retailers experienced an intense compound annual growth rate (CAGR) from 1995 to 2001: Home Depot grew at 22.6 percent, Albertson's at 28.8 percent, Kroger at 15.6 percent, among others. Famed businessman Jack Welch once said, "If the rate of change on the outside exceeds the rate of change on the inside, the end is near." Considering the fact that Sears grew at 3.1 percent and K-Mart at 1.3 percent over this same period,[4] are the problems that these brands have had over the subsequent years at all surprising?

More to the point at hand: Why is the consolidation of the retail environment a problem for magazines? A quick look at the industry supply chain helps explain this. Traditionally, the structure of the magazine publishing industry began with the publisher—in this case, Time, Inc.—and ended with the retailer that sells the magazines to consumers. In between the two, however, is where the lessons reside. Specifically, in 1995, *Time* took 56 percent off the cover price of a magazine. Each publisher has a distribution arm attached to it (for example, TDS, which serviced *Time*, Meredith, and Condé Nast; and Warner Publishing Services servicing Warner Publishing, Ziff Davis, and others). These distribution services don't actually physically distribute the magazines and, contractually, they collect 4 percent of the cover price of any Time, Inc. publication. The distributor works with the publisher and decides, based on a variety of factors including time of year and the content's newsworthiness, how many copies to have printed. In turn, wholesalers pick up the shrink-wrapped packages of magazines at the print shop and distribute them to the various retail outlets. In 1995, these wholesalers were taking about 20 percent of the revenue from the magazines' cover price. Finally, the increasingly powerful and consolidated retailer took approximately 20 percent of the cover price.

Breakdown of 1995 Revenue per Cover Sold	
Publisher (e.g., Time, Inc.)	56%
Distributor (e.g., TDS, WPS)	4%
Wholesaler (e.g., Anderson, Hudson)	20%
Retailer (e.g., Walmart)	20%

To understand the evolution of this industry, examining the industry's structure was crucial. The publishers at the top of the supply chain and the retailers at the other end were both consolidated and powerful; anyone who has ever competed and/ or negotiated with Walmart or Time can attest to this. The TDS division of Time received its place in the supply chain according to the contract established with Time, Inc., the publisher. By contrast, the wholesaler segment in 1995 was very fragmented. Five geographically concentrated wholesalers—Anderson, News Group, Unimag, Charles Levy, and Hudson—held 30 percent of the market. The other 70 percent was controlled by small, regional players.

Quick Quiz #1: Can you predict what would happen by 2005 as magazine retailers consolidate?

Answer: As the retailers grew, they put increasing price pressure on the channel. The powerful publishers and their contractually tied distribution arm pushed back. This left only one place in the channel to give: the wholesalers stuck in the middle.

It was a bloodbath. The five geographically concentrated wholesalers with 30 percent of the market became four players—those named above minus Unimag—and now controlled 90 percent of the market. Most of the small regional players were forced to fold following a slew of bankruptcies.

2005 Revenue per Cover Sold	
Publisher (e.g., Time, Inc.)	53%
Distributor (e.g., TDS, WPS)	4%
Wholesaler (e.g., Anderson, Hudson)	14%
Retailer (e.g., Walmart)	29%

Key Lesson: If you were a wholesaler back in 1995, and you were not either getting bigger (that is, consolidating and trying to take advantage of scale economies) or finding something else to do for a living (exiting the industry), then I have no clue what you were thinking. Actually, it is clear that people in such situations weren't thinking. And the failure to think strategically here and plan for the future was a recipe for financial ruin in this environment. It was abundantly clear given the data in 1995 that the wholesalers would be getting squeezed between the powerful publishers at the top and the increasingly powerful (and consolidating) retailers at the end of the chain. Hence, you would need to grow to gain scale, cut costs, and try to gain leverage in the channel to be sustainable. Gaining scale was essential.

And it is no different today. The lesson—the analogy to your business—is as follows: Let's say someone looked back on your business today from 10 or 15 years in the future and imagine you didn't do X, leading others to ask: "What in the heck were they thinking, they didn't do X?!" The question for you is: What would X be? These are the new disruptive technologies, the structural elements, the inevitabilities that—if you don't address now—will leave you in the market's dust. You'd be the metaphorical equivalent of the wholesalers that weren't growing in size in 1995.

This situation is playing out again within the publishing industry today: those that fail to heed history's lessons are doomed to repeat it. It isn't consolidation that is transforming the publishing industry today; it isn't even the increased use of the Internet *per se*. It is the fact that two behemoths—Apple and Amazon—now own the majority of the industry supply chain for digital publishing. Both realized a long time ago that gaining control here could be *highly* lucrative and would enable them to leverage strengths in ways that no one could match. If one could own the primary source by which users obtained books and other items online (Amazon.com), control the content distribution (the Kindle store) and the device (the Kindle), one could exert pressure upstream to the authors and publishers, thereby extracting a higher percentage of the margins (not unlike Walmart did in the previous example). By locking down the distribution chain, Amazon CEO Jeff Bezos knew that he'd be able to extract margins throughout and exert pressure up the chain—and gain an extraordinarily powerful advantage.

Amazon knew that others, such as Barnes & Noble, would try to do the same, but it didn't count on the fact that Apple CEO Steve Jobs would recognize this opportunity as well. While Barnes & Noble knew that the market for brick and mortar book distribution could eventually only support, at most, one larger player (hence, Borders' fate), it has tried to address the distribution end with its Nook and related online activities. This could have been an incredibly effective strategy were it not for Amazon's and Apple's control of the distribution chain for not only publishing, but also a whole host of other items. This has left Barnes & Noble at the mercy of the deals that Apple and Amazon have negotiated. As the world increasingly moves to digital distribution of content, these two big players will only become more important in this space, hence, the intense battle between them. Have you ever tried to buy a book through your Kindle app on your iPhone or iPad? You can't. Apple wants a cut of this transaction, and Amazon won't allow it. The dispute is not at all surprising given the potential impact of these moves for writers, publishers, and consumers, alike.

MP3.com, Apple, Sony and Lessons Learned Today

MP3.com was a start-up founded by entrepreneurs Michael Robertson and Greg Flores in the heart of the dot-com boom. The rise of digital technologies paved the way for companies like music sharing site Napster and companies like MP3.com that mixed old with new. MP3.com let customers place online orders for custom CDs from start-up bands as well as some established talent. In what was the largest technology IPO to date, MP3.com went public on July 21, 1999. Although it had mostly been a venue for lesser known and indie artists to get their music out, bigger names participated and owned a significant post-IPO stake. At its peak, MP3.com delivered over 4 million MP3-formatted audio files per day to over 800,000 unique users on a customer base of 25 million registered users.[5]

On January 12, 2000, MP3.com launched a service that enabled users to securely register their personal CDs and then stream digital copies online. Since consumers could only listen online to music they already owned, MP3.com saw this as a revenue opportunity. Unfortunately, the record industry did not see it that way. It sued MP3.com, claiming, "The service constituted unauthorized duplication and promoted copyright infringement." MP3.com lost this case and was eventually purchased by Vivendi Universal in May of 2001 for $5 a share—significantly below its IPO launch price of $28 per share.

There are many lessons inherent in this story. But the most important for us is who eventually won this battle. Ask yourself: would you have paid $28—or $105—a share back in July 1999?

> *Quick Quiz #2*: Who would you have predicted had the right to win in the market for the digital transmission of music at the turn of the millennium?
>
> *Answer*: Two logical answers would be Sony, and perhaps an industry content owner such as Universal Music. Sony had all

the elements—its Walkman line of products, a catalog of music, and artists under contract to its record label. The record labels could potentially boost slowing CD sales by shifting revenue generation from expensive physical retail distribution to lower-cost online operations.

Why, then, was this market's *real* winner a *computer* company—one without any presence in portable mobile devices *or* music? Thanks largely to the genius of Steve Jobs, Apple Computer recognized many things about this industry. But what may have been most important was what it didn't recognize: its need to protect its existing business since it had none in this area. On the other hand, Universal and other record companies were concerned with protecting their intellectual property—the music and artists. They were scared silly that they'd lose their lock on distribution. So they sued and usually won. However, while they were suing the myriad of Internet-based start-ups like MP3.com and Napster, Apple was in the process of eating their lunch.

It was no different for Sony. Because of the company's perceived need to protect its record division's intellectual property and related corporate infighting, the systems Sony introduced to digital music were arcane and difficult to use. And even though it launched a few innovative products, its recording interface and processes were incredibly non-intuitive and clumsy to use.[6] Sony was so concerned with protecting its music's copyright that it failed to make its interface user-friendly. Clearly, this opened the door for someone who did make things easy for users to seize the market. Enter Steve Jobs.

It is interesting to note that the winner in the market for digital music transmission is the one firm that recognized just this: if you control the key strategic control points in the industry and own the interface, all else follows suit. Despite the changes that have taken place over the years, this remains the same. And again, those that fail to heed the lessons of history are doomed to repeat it.

The Lesson: work outside in, not inside out. Recognize customer needs first and then work to deliver solutions. *Never* create an offering that meets internal constituents' needs and then try to deliver *this* offering to market. Steve Jobs recognized his customers' desires first and above all else. In contrast, Sony recognized a key emerging trend, but delivered offerings based on what its internal team deemed essential to protect the intellectual property of its record division, not what the buying public wanted.

Chapter Summary and Key Business Principles

- The external business environment is all of those things you cannot control. Universal Music was not about to stop the tide of the Internet and digital transmission of music through lawsuits.
- Think through and map out the external business environment. Fail to do so at your peril. Always ask: What external factors will drive your market moving forward?
- Work through distribution and the industry's supply chain to spot trends, opportunities, and potential areas of vulnerability.
- Assess market opportunity space critically; use formal metrics to assess size, growth, and margin opportunities.
- Beware the typical innovator's Rizzutoism: trying to find a market for an invention rather than finding an innovation for a market need.
- Avoid:
  - Purely cost-driven decisions. This is only one of many factors to consider.
  - Lack of attention to history. Remember: those that ignore its lessons are doomed to repeat it.

- Arrogance. At all costs. Enough said.
- Hope. Hope is not a strategy.
- The all-in decision: betting everything on a risky proposition. Always plan for contingencies and mitigate risk.

Key Business Tools

- External market analysis
- Distribution and competitive supply chain analysis
- Thinking outside in, not inside out

CHAPTER 3

Managing the Risk of Growth

The importance of growing from the core—expansion into
adjacent markets.

—The Story of Captain Jepp and Jeppesen's
Expansion into the Marine Environment[1]

W e begin this chapter by discussing a key issue for managing the risk of growth—growing from the core:

Core defined: The set of products, capabilities, customers, channels, and geographies that defines the essence of the company and fulfills its vision statement and mission.

In short, the core is what a company does today—the essence of its business. Growth and expansion away from this core can take place across multiple potential avenues or steps by doing such things as:

- Expanding into new products and/or services to existing customers
- Entering new geographies with existing offerings
- Addressing new customer segments
- Expanding along the industry supply chain
- Using new distribution channels

As you move ever further away from your current core business, you are less and less likely to succeed. To illustrate, a study conducted a few years ago demonstrates how difficult it is to expand in multiple directions away from the core (see Figure 3.1).[2] The researchers counted the absence of five items to define how far a move is away from the core—shared customers, shared costs, shared channels, shared competitors, and shared capabilities and technology—and then added them up. For example, lacking shared customers and costs would be a two-step move. Success rates are low even at a one-step adjacent move; once you're at more than three, new venture success rates fall below 10 percent on average. Simply stated, as you move into increasingly unfamiliar territory, it becomes increasingly difficult to succeed.

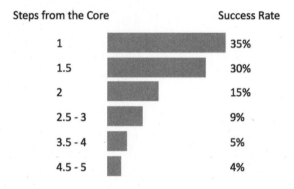

Measuring distance from core; e.g., if the new venture lacks one of the below element, it is one step away from the core
- Level of shared customers
- Level of shared costs
- Level of shared channels
- Level of shared competitors
- Level of shared capabilities and technology

Steps from the Core	Success Rate
1	35%
1.5	30%
2	15%
2.5 - 3	9%
3.5 - 4	5%
4.5 - 5	4%

Figure 3.1 Chance of success falls dramatically as you move further from the core.

Some Examples of Successes and Failure Expanding from the Core[3]

Success: expanding one step at a time. Nike is perhaps the most often cited example of a company that has grown sequentially one step at a time from its core. First, it expanded sales of its athletic shoes geographically across North America and then one step at a time into international markets. Subsequent moves focused on new sports one step at a time, first into basketball (with Michael Jordan) and then into golf (with Tiger Woods). From new geographies to new sports to athletic apparel to distribution, Nike has demonstrated repeatedly how companies can succeed by expanding from the core into sequential adjacent markets. Similar success stories are numerous: IBM's move into services that built on its core computer business; Xerox is currently moving to services related to its core in office automation; Virgin Airlines has expanded from the United Kingdom and Europe to the U.S. market; Starbucks expanded first to new geographies, then to new product lines, and then to different retail growth avenues through supermarkets.

Failure: expanding multiple steps at once. Cisco's "Flip Flop with Flip" provides a graphic example of a company attempting too many simultaneous steps away from its core. Cisco bought the Flip camera business for $590 million in 2008, and then shuttered the business in early 2011, taking a $300 million tax write-off and laying off 550 workers. The retail camera business was at least four steps from its networking core—few shared customers, partially shared channels, similar geographies, few shared competitors and very few shared capabilities and technologies. The only surprising—and truly unfortunate—part is that it took Cisco three years and $300 million to figure this out. Similarly, Boeing's Connexion by Boeing (CBB) business was launched in 2004, providing Internet service aboard commercial planes beginning with Lufthansa flights out of Germany. The business did not succeed for various reasons, one of which was that Boeing's core is in the business-to-business side of the aviation industry. The company had little competency in running a retail service delivered to the flying passenger rather than the airline itself. In stark contrast, Internet delivery in the air has proved successful for Gogo Internet, a start-up whose core was delivering retail.

While it is possible to draw the conclusion that it's not *necessary* to stay close to the core, any move away from it should be taken with caution. It's also preferable to make sequential moves to larger multiple steps that occur at any one point in time.

A textbook example of how to do this over time is that of the aviation navigation company Jeppesen. The company started with the aerial maps created by Elrey B. Jeppesen, known as "Captain Jepp"—a larger-than-life character back in his day (which you can get a feel for if you visit Jeppesen's headquarters in Colorado and see the black-and-white pictures of him picnicking with Amelia Earhart and "wing walking" on biplanes).

When Captain Jepp began charting the routes, he was 24 years old and had joined Boeing Air Transport (BAT) as an airmail pilot.[4] At the time, he was "just trying to stay alive" by avoiding obstacles using his maps. In those days, pilots did not have anything in the way of charts except for Rand McNally road maps. They flew anywhere from 50 to 300 feet above the ground, navigating mostly by terrain features and "dead reckoning," following railroad tracks in bad weather. They often flew along the Union Pacific railroad tracks, doing what became known as "hugging the UP." Jeppesen recounted, "It was rough flying over those mountains. You'd fly from one emergency field to the next . . . [often sitting] until the storm passed, [waiting to] go on." He continued, "Out of the 18 pilots flying the Cheyenne to Salt Lake hitch, four were killed in the line of duty during the winter of 1930—a dear price to pay for pioneering. That's when I wised up!" Jeppesen began drawing airfield charts not to make money, but more "to preserve myself for old age and to help fellow pilots."

The original manual that Captain Jepp started came about from him "climbing mountains and smokestacks. I just started writing it all down." He eventually traveled from Chicago to Oakland, checking out emergency fields and obstructions, different ways to get around them, how far they were from the railway track and the highway. At first, he gave copies of his "Little Black Book" to his friends. Soon the demand became so great that he began selling them. When low-frequency radio beacons became available in 1931, Captain Jepp updated his black book to show pilots how to follow them. He added mileage reference charts and terrain elevation profiles. He founded Jeppesen & Company in 1934, initially setting up shop in his basement workshop in Salt Lake City, Utah, where he created his first instrument flying charts.

United Airlines decided to use Jeppesen's charts throughout its organization, becoming one of the first airlines to subscribe to his early Airway Manual Service. In 1941, he moved his company to Denver and expanded services to include flight information publications for the U.S. Navy and customers in the commercial air transportation business. Six years later, Jeppesen and the Federal Aviation Administration developed and introduced Standard Instrument Approach Procedures and established the U.S. National Flight Data Center.

Jeppesen's first international expansion began in 1957 when he set up an office to provide services to customers in Europe. In 1973, the first commercial flight used Jeppesen's proprietary NavData® system using inertial navigation systems, eventually leading to the satellite-based Global Positioning System (GPS).

Jeppesen's expansion into adjacent markets began in 1974, when they undertook a strategy to complement his navigation and charting tools one step at a time. To this end, the 1980s and 1990s saw Jeppesen acquiring companies and capabilities and growing into global markets. During this time, Jeppesen expanded to attract customers in vertical and adjacent market segments in textbook fashion. Because new opportunities in the traditional aerospace market segment were limited—and could not come close to meeting the necessary revenue growth targets—Jeppesen looked to adjacent markets for growth, as many companies do.

Jeppesen's expansion is a classic example of a company that knew the importance of growing first in its core and then into adjacent markets. It began with its core commercial airline customers, first providing navigation solutions and then adding products to the portfolio over time, one at a time: operations, document solutions, software solutions and route planning and eventually training service and support. From there, the company expanded from delivering these services to major airline customers to offering them to the general and business aviation segments, then to the military, and eventually to the marine space—one market at a time.

This example illustrates how to effectively grow into adjacent markets one step at a time. Jeppesen built a portfolio of offerings for its major airline customers and then grew these offerings into new markets: general and business aviation, government and military, and then eventually to marine. Such a strategy leverages a company's core competencies, skills, and mission into new markets in a way that minimizes the inherent risks usually associated with such category jumps.

It also emphasizes the need for a reasoned process. It's vital that you first assess where you are currently versus where you should be in the long run—and appropriately expand horizontally and sequentially over time. From here, you can leverage strengths across your core markets to expand into attractive vertical markets where appropriate. The classic example of this is Nike's expansion into adjacent sports markets (basketball and golf from athletic shoes). More recent examples include Starbucks expanding to an additional retail space (the grocery store) and Avis expanding into the short-term rental space through its acquisition of Zipcar.

For your company, the process of assessing proximity to the core is a straightforward, albeit important one. It does not determine your strategic direction, but it's an outstanding first step at assessing precisely how risky your strategy may be—one that alerts you quickly to ways to minimize or mitigate risks.

Exercise: Assessing Your Potential Move
Away from the Core

As such, a good template to follow the logic of the core is as follows. Imagine you have a new offering in mind for your business, one that you see as a new growth opportunity or perhaps the latest trend. How risky is it for you to stretch to new territory?

In order to assess this, answer the questions below, where every "yes" answer gets a score of 0 and every "no" answer gets a score of 1. Since this is reality and reality is not black and white, you can allow for partial scores. So, for example, if the offering were in a combination of new and existing customers, then a score of 0.5 for Question 4 would be perfectly reasonable.

Write Score Below

Question 1: Does this new offering utilize existing capabilities and technologies?_____

Question 2: Will you be competing against the same set of competitors that you do now?_____

Question 3: Does this new offering have significant cost overlap with existing offerings, perhaps via shared inputs, components, or plants?_____

Question 4: Will you be selling to the same set of customers that you currently are?_____

Question 5: Will you be selling through the same channels as you are currently?_____

Total:_____

How did you do (note that expanding to new geographies, while not explicitly listed here, is covered in questions 2, 4, and, in part, question 3)? Based on the work by Zook and

(continued)

(*continued*)

Allen—see Figure 3.1—we know that, on average, across multiple industries:

If your score was:	Your probability of success is:
Equal to 1 or less	35%
Equal to 1.5	30%
Equal to 2	15%
Between 2.5 and 3	9%
Between 3.5 and 4	5%
Between 4.5 and 5	4%

These percentages aren't exactly encouraging. Be careful if you are saying, "yes, but we are different . . ." As in the example of the corner restaurants that failed one after the other, we all too often think we're different. Instead of arrogantly thinking you're different, critically assess (1) is this new opportunity worth the risk, (2) if it is, are there ways to minimize, mitigate or diversify away the risk, are there potential "off ramps" to take if certain milestones aren't attained, and (3) can we take this one step at a time with the same outcome but lower risk? Don't just use this as a guide; take it seriously. Try to think Nike, not Cisco's ill-fated foray into Flip!

Lessons from Jeppesen for Businesses Wanting to Grow and Expand into Adjacent Markets

- Grow from your core—but first and foremost, *get your core right.* If your core is weak, it will be exceedingly difficult to succeed in new markets.
- Success depends in large part upon *how far from the core* the growth opportunity rests. The further away you are, the more difficult it becomes.

- If you have the luxury of time, *growing sequentially* over time, one step at a time, has a higher overall likelihood of success.

- If entry into an adjacent market further away from your core is time sensitive, *be honest about your competencies* versus those of your potential competitors. This will allow you to appropriately assess and find ways to mitigate the risk of expansion.

- Don't be paralyzed by fear of moves that are too far away from your immediate core; but *be prudent*. Companies do succeed with moves away from the core, but they are the exception rather than the rule.

- Don't follow the "Corner Restaurant Rizzutoism" and bet the farm on a move far away from the core. Be sure *you are able to lose your investment* should the move fail. Diversify and be cautious.

Of course, this whole discussion is predicated on the need to grow. So why *do* we place such an emphasis on growth? We revisit that famous quote from Jack Welch noted earlier for the answer:

"When the rate of change inside an institution becomes slower than the rate of change outside, the end is in sight. The only question is when."

When rivals are growing faster than you are, they gain the advantage in terms of scale economies, learning economies, marketing, and R&D spend efficiencies. Simply put, if your competitors are growing at a faster pace over time, it's just a matter of when—not if—they will have advantages that are insurmountable. However, you also have to be careful how you grow. Straying too far from the core can be hazardous to a company's financial health; to this end, beware the inevitable urge to think "we're different," as all of those that failed before believed.

The next chapter addresses the crucial building blocks for competing in the right space—the critical component in assessing *where to grow*. It is also a critical part of the decision process that leads to an assessment as to whether we can grow organically or inorganically through a merger or acquisition. Indeed, the strategic part of M&A

activity—usually done prior to financial due diligence—is conducted during the M&A process outlined in the following section. This is precisely why value chain analysis is a fundamental building block of strategy for both organic and engineered growth—and for discerning what competencies you may need to acquire. In short, before we can decide *how* to compete, we need to decide *where* to compete. Far too many companies focus on how well they are competing in their existing markets, when this may not even be a relevant factor—especially if they're competing well in a part of the market with low margins or where someone else is doing better. Doing a great job in a bad market is still bad business—and will always be a bad business proposition.

The "New Math" or Inorganic Growth

1. $2 + 2 = 5$ (on the revenue side)
2. $2 + 2 = 3$ (on the cost side)
3. $730 = 365$ (in terms of speed to market)

The logic displayed above pertains to strategic reasons why firms may choose to grow via acquisition, often referred to as "inorganic" since growth is not driven internally (organically). The logic is straightforward: there are really only three reasons for an acquisition: (1) $2 + 2 = 5$ on the revenue side, (2) $2 + 2 = 3$ on the cost side, or (3) it increases speed to market and pulls revenue forward as opposed to growing organically. Simply put, if a potential acquisition doesn't achieve cost savings, revenue synergies, or reduce time to market, there may be little reason to do the acquisition. Value chain analysis is often central to the M&A decision from a strategic perspective and can help in identifying the relationships that are central to any strategy. To this, the book now turns.

Chapter Summary and Key Business Principles

- Growth and expansion happens away from the core, across multiple potential avenues or steps:
  - Expand into new products and/or services to existing customers.
  - Enter new geographies with existing offerings.
  - Address new customer segments.
  - Expand along the value chain.
  - Use new distribution channels.
- Success rates fall precipitously for offerings that are further away from the core.
- Process steps to follow in practice are:
  - Assess the value chain (discussed in more detail later).
  - Modify position in the value chain (vertical expansion).
  - Modify along horizontal dimensions where appropriate (horizontal expansion).
  - Always focus on the long run.

Key Business Tools

- Core versus adjacent markets
- Expansion along the core through the value chain
- Understanding the strategic rationale for mergers and acquisitions—the "new math" of acquisitions

Choosing and Competing Effectively in the Right Space

Competing in the right space—the value chain and strategic control points
> — William Sheppard, Minnetonka, Crème Soap on Tap
> and the story of the pumps

I n this chapter, we develop in detail two critical building blocks for creating effective strategy: strategic control points and the value chain. We first illustrate the definition of a strategic control point via an example. Perhaps the best—and most dramatic—example is that of widely used liquid hand soap Softsoap®.

Back in 1865, William Sheppard of New York was granted a patent of "Improved Liquid Soap." His invention was a good one with many practical uses, but like many inventions, it did not make its way into people's homes until many years after he conceived it. It wasn't until 1980, in fact, that the Minnetonka Corporation started offering "Crème Soap on Tap" through boutique distributors. The product was a success, and the corporation decided to follow up with a similar product for mass retail sale.[1]

During the launch, the company decided to package the product in a distinctive looking pump bottle. The problem, however, for this relatively small producer of consumer goods (and for countless others), was that retailing is intensely competitive. There are requirements to get on the shelves ("slotting allowances") and performance guarantees ("failure fees") once on the shelves. Both are tough barriers for a small manufacturer to overcome, especially one that faced potentially overwhelming competition from giants such as Procter & Gamble, Johnson & Johnson, Colgate-Palmolive, and Unilever. In short, the best Minnetonka could hope for was to be a huge success on the shelves and even this would invite swift and formidable—perhaps even insurmountable—competition. On the other hand, Minnetonka believed that having at least a six-month lead on potential competitors would allow it build up enough of a brand presence and shelf space allocation that it would be able to maintain at least a one-third market share—even after the "big boys" entered. So, how does one gain a six-month lead over potential entrants, that is, how does one forestall others' entry into a market? The answer lies with the notion of strategic control points.

In short, Minnetonka decided to buy up the world's supply of plastic pumps. By doing this, any other manufacturers that wanted to enter the liquid soap market would have to wait until the supply was replenished or build their own factories to make the pumps. That process would take at least six to eight months, which was the amount of time Minnetonka needed to build distribution, shelf allocation, and a brand presence. The result was a hugely successful Softsoap® brand, one that was bought out by Colgate-Palmolive in 1987.

In this instance, pump manufacturing was a classic strategic control point—a part of the supply chain that, if controlled, enabled Minnetonka to gain a differential competitive advantage in the key part of the market that it was after: retail. Note that there may or may not be a potentially profitable business in pump manufacturing; however, controlling that part of the process was a critical part of making the profitable part happen. And, as they say, the rest is history.

The Story of the Agricultural Chemical Manufacturer and the Helicopter Pilot

A second example of a strategic control point is in the area of agricultural chemicals back in the late 2000s. In forestry, chemicals are used to ensure that the right kinds of trees grow and to retard the growth of the underbrush. There are major chemical manufacturers such as DuPont, Syngenta, and BASF that dominate the market for forestry chemicals. Of these, BASF is the largest with, historically, about an 80 percent market share on the forestry side of the business.

As depicted in Figure 4.1 the chemicals are sold to end users (such as large land owners, utility companies) through distributors and applicators. The distributors typically own the relationship with the end user

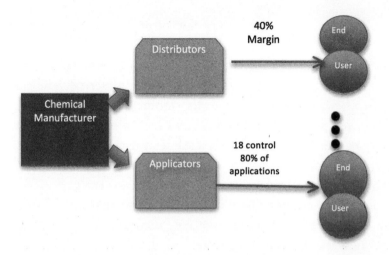

Figure 4.1   Structure of the market for chemicals used in forestry in the late 2000s in the United States.

and take a substantial margin, close to 40 percent. For years, these manufacturers wanted to bypass the distributors and go directly to end users, thereby forgoing the need to pay these margins. The applicators are firms that run helicopters across large tracts of land. These helicopter pilots require specialized skills; it can take two years to train a pilot with an existing helicopter license to be able to operate a helicopter for this purpose. Partially as a result, there were 18 helicopter firms that controlled over 80 percent of the coverage in U.S. forestry markets, and they remained idle as much as 25 percent of the time.

So, knowing all this, how could the chemical manufacturers have used the notion of strategic control points to bypass the distributors? The answer is simple: they could offer to buy up the helicopter pilots' "tach time" (time in the air)—even at a premium, at above market rates—for more than 100 percent of available time.

Sign up the applicators so that they have no available tach time left for anyone else (especially for the distributors), and you squeeze the distributors out. As stated before, they will need at least two years in order to train helicopter pilots with sufficient skills to be up and running. Very few, if any, of the distributors would be able to withstand multiple years without revenue while simultaneously developing helicopter talent, operations, and, well, helicopters. The manufacturers would effectively be able to bypass the distributors; cut costs significantly, thereby being able to lower prices; and, given that there was no harm—only benefit—at the customer level, escape antitrust intervention. Thus, the helicopter firms, the applicators, are a classic example of a strategic control point in this market.

So, one might ask: why *hasn't* this been done in practice? In the interest of presenting a fair and complete picture, this isn't the only market where the distributors allocate product. Therefore, a move by one of this market's big manufacturers would undoubtedly prompt distributors in, say, the aquatics market to make a retaliatory move. Hence, companies do need to consider cross-market effects (but this would make for a less interesting and clean example here). Nonetheless, it does beg the question: Why isn't there more consolidation on the applicator side? One would expect this to take place moving forward, much like we saw in the Time example in Chapter 2. Should this happen, distributors beware.

Legacy Frameworks: The Industry's Supply Chain

The concept of an industry supply chain was developed decades ago—its origins date back to the Leontief Input-Output Model, developed by Harvard professor Wassily Leontief in the 1950s, which earned its creator the Nobel Prize in Economics in 1973. In its simplest form, this concept of the industry supply chain is a physical representation of the various processes involved in producing goods and services, creating flow from raw materials on through to delivery, service, and support of the final offering in the market.[2]

While inherently "siloed" in design and process-oriented, this concept can provide a very useful sense of where value is created in

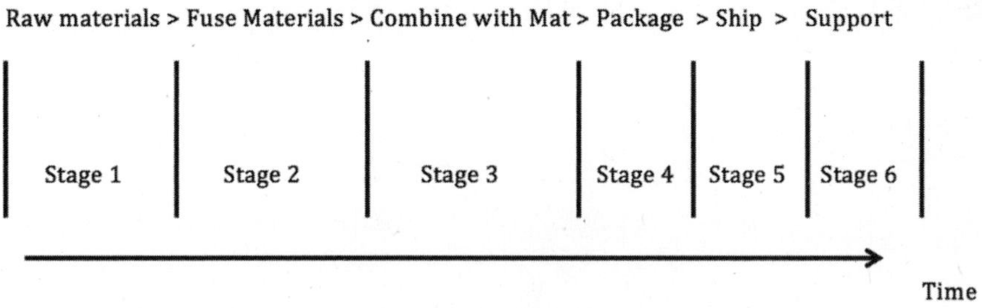

Raw materials > Fuse Materials > Combine with Mat > Package > Ship > Support

| Stage 1 | Stage 2 | Stage 3 | Stage 4 | Stage 5 | Stage 6 |

Time

Figure 4.2   Value Chain Flow.

the supply chain in a given industry. For example, plotting a first-level (simple) supply chain for asphalt shingles to be used on the roofs of buildings might look something like Figure 4.2.

Understanding where value is created throughout the supply chain—and where companies can make additional gains in terms of efficiency or margin extraction—can provide valuable insight to a firm operating in this space. One very convenient, visual way to convey the value that may be captured is by tracing the source of revenue at each stage in the value chain. Imagine a firm in the software delivery business whose high-level value chain consists of collecting data, writing software and the visual interface, distributing the product to customers, and then providing after-sales service and support. We can capture the value throughout the value chain as follows:

The hypothetical example of the software firm in Figure 4.3 makes it extremely clear where the sweet spot—at least in terms of margin—is in the value chain. In this example, it is in the area of service and support (top right).

The Value Chain, Strategic Control Points, and Competency Gaps—Jeppesen's Expansion into the Marine Environment

Jeppesen, Inc. has a rich history in aviation mapping and navigation. Since the 1930s, it has provided charts for the vast majority of commercial flights around the world, continuing the tradition

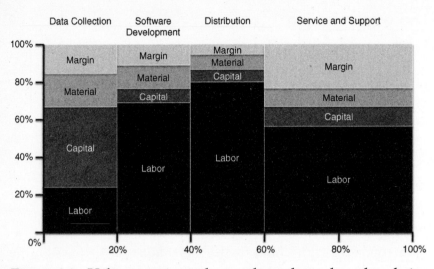

Figure 4.3 Value, margin, and costs throughout the value chain, hypothetical example, software.

started by company founder Captain Jepp back in the 1930s as discussed in Chapter 3. In 2005, Jeppesen was considering entering an adjacent market—the digital marine navigation market (think large shippers such as Maersk on blue- and brown-water routes or tragedies such as the *Exxon Valdez* in Alaska or the *Concordia* laying on its side in the Mediterranean off the coast of Italy).[3] As it turns out, virtually all of the world's marine charting was still done using paper in 2005. Hence, Jeppesen wanted to enter this market by focusing on transforming standard paper charts into digital format. The company had considerable expertise in aviation, route planning and optimization, and operations research, in addition to digitizing and presenting maps and navigation aids electronically. However, it knew little about the marine market. So this was essentially a three-step adjacency, since it had no shared customers, channels, or competitors. And this suggested taking a caution approach (remember Figure 3.1 presented in Chapter 3: three-step adjacent moves have less than a 10 percent probability of success).

So, how might Jeppesen have used the framework described previously to analyze the potential entry decision? In particular, what are the key strategic control points? Should the company enter organically or through acquisition? What risks does it need to address with regard to mitigation plans and the like?

To illustrate, a competitive and capabilities map is constructed in two stages, with the first laying out the value chain and key strategic control points. In order to enter the digital navigation market, Jeppesen needed to access maritime data (currently in paper form) then digitize, mine, and fuse the data in digitized form. It then had to write a graphical user interface (GUI—think Windows or the Mac OS interface), get access to the bridge of the ship and the ship's systems data, integrate the software onto the ship's system, transmit the data including updates, and provide after-purchase service and support.

There were two things that Jeppesen absolutely needed in order to enter the market for digital marine navigation: (1) the maritime charts/data and (2) access to the real estate on the bridge of the ship (that is, they needed to get their offering, in whatever form, onto the bridge).[4] The United Kingdom Hydrographic Office (UKHO) owned the rights to the vast majority of the existing official data on the world's international waterways (though other companies had compiled unofficial data). Without obtaining access to chart data, it would be impossible for Jeppesen to enter the market at all. If, on the other hand, it was able to obtain *exclusive* access to the official UKHO data, it would own a key strategic control point when the move from paper to digital charts became mandated in phases starting in 2012.[5] Alternatively, if a potential competitor were able to obtain exclusive access to the official data and, in turn, turn it into digital format, Jeppesen faced the possibility of being frozen out of the market entirely when the digital mandate kicked in.

Second, and even more important, any company that was able to gain access to the bridge of the major shippers and integrate software into the ship's existing onboard systems, including route and fuel optimization, could potentially exclude rivals, since it's impractical to have two different fuel optimization software programs running simultaneously on board a ship. A company could also charge monopoly rents on bridge access and integration for fuel savings, which was the real sweet spot in this market. Note that for this part of the market (fuel and route optimization), access to the official data wasn't necessarily crucial—Jeppesen could in principal optimize fuel consumption without the maritime data—for this, access to the bridge of the ship was the critical point of strategic control. Thus, the two key control points in this industry were, for very different reasons, data access and bridge access.

Any firm that could dominate in these two areas—lock up data access and/or bridge access for key customers—would succeed in this market and could leverage this strength by pushing higher margins through the space. It could also have been a source of failure; lack of success in locking up these two key strategic control points—or worse yet, a competitor locking up one or both—meant this would no longer be a viable business. Hence, Jeppesen focused all of its launch plans—and risk mitigation potential off-ramps—on these two control points.

The value chain that Jeppesen faced upon entering the marine space can also be mapped against capabilities—of Jeppesen and of its rivals—in order to assess gaps that may exist. In Figure 4.4, solid denotes strong capabilities, while checkered suggests that only some capabilities are present; and gray represents weak or no capabilities. The value chain is mapped along the top row and the set of potential competitors (or acquisition targets) is listed in the left-hand column.

Ideally, Jeppesen would have strong core competencies in the key areas of strategic control, and most or all of its competitors would not. In part, this is what we look for in developing profitable areas in which to compete: areas of potential strategic control in the value chain where we bring unique capabilities to the space, ones that none of our competitors can match.

● High ▨ Medium/Inconsistent ○ Weak/None

Value Chain	Legacy Market				Digital Future			
	Data		Application		Distribution			
Value Chain (Details)	Source Data	Mine Data	Fusion (Application)	Software Code	Paper Distribution	Network Distribution	Access (Hardware)	Product Interface
Level of Strategic Control	High	Low	Low	Low	Low	High		
Capabilities Required	Relationship with data owners	Data mining and cataloging software	Algorithm	Software development expertise	Printing, packaging shipping	Distribution network, hardware access, certification authority (SOLAS)		
Jeppesen Marine								
UK Hydrographic Organization/NOAA/NGA/USCS/USACE								
C-Map (Recreational)								
Navonics (Recreational/Coastal)								
IIC								
Seven C's								

Figure 4.4 Competitive and Capabilities Map.

Figure 4.4 highlights what would be a strategic nightmare—Jeppesen lacked competencies in the two main areas of strategic control, whereas it had critical competencies in important areas (data fusion and digital mapping and optimization), but not key strategic control points. That is, even if the company was "world class" in these areas, someone else who owned the data and/or real estate on the ship's bridge could freeze it out of the market (or, at a minimum, squeeze margins out of the channel). Hence, unless Jeppesen was able to obtain competencies in these two key areas, entry would likely be unsuccessful.

This leads to the critical strategic question facing Jeppesen at the time: should it attempt to obtain these competencies organically (in other words, develop them in-house) or inorganically (through acquisition)? If we examine Figure 4.4 more closely, we can see that two companies—C-Map and Navionics—had capabilities in both strategic control points, making them natural acquisition targets. This is one of the reasons Jeppesen acquired C-Map in 2007; quite often, strategic analysis of this type is used as the first cut at M&A analysis (if a potential target fills key strategic capabilities, the next step is the financial due diligence to assess the financial viability of the target). Once Jeppesen gained access to the two key strategic control points, its next objective was to strengthen its ability to deliver the part of the value chain that could potentially post the best margins: vessel and voyage optimization solutions (VVOS) for fuel efficiency by purchasing Ocean Systems, Inc. (OSI), a company specializing in VVOS systems. It now offers a full suite of products consistent with a variety of customer needs across segments.

Strategic Exercise

Draw the high-level value chain for the industry in which you operate. From this, answer the following:

- Are there areas of the value chain that have the potential to be a strategic control point?
- Do you have competencies in these areas?
- Do your competitors have competencies in these areas?
- Are there specific parts of the value chain that have the potential for strategic control where you have competitive advantage and where your competitors do not?
- Are there specific parts of the value chain that have the potential for strategic control where your competitors have competitive advantage and where you do not?

In your industry, the key is finding areas of potential strategic control where you have competitive advantage and using them to your advantage. What are they in your industry?

Hence, Jeppesen's path of expansion follows an almost textbook route to market: recognizing the market's key strategic control points and developing capabilities in these areas (in this instance through acquisition) and staying close to the core on each sequential move. Then, once these capabilities were in place, it focused on strengthening the areas of the value chain (in this case, VVOS) with the best potential for margin extraction, and leveraging strength in this part of the market to extract margins throughout the chain.

Finally, it may be helpful to think of this in reverse. That is, had Jeppesen not been able to succeed in getting access to the real estate on board the ship, it wouldn't have benefited from VVOS competency acquisition through the OSI acquisition. Further, had it been able to develop these capabilities in-house (organically), it wouldn't have needed to acquire C-Map. And while organic development may have been possible here, the timing was crucial. Being first to market and generating subscription revenue as soon as possible was essential to financial success in a market that was about to transition quickly from paper to digital. Jeppesen simply couldn't wait for these capabilities to grow organically.

Here, speed to market in terms of accessing the key strategic control points was crucial, echoing a point made earlier—being first is often critical when you are seeking to obtain a strategic control point. In contrast, entering first with a product that has inherently imitable features usually means that any strategic advantage may be fleeting. This distinction is crucial: Being first to market with a strategic control point is often sustainable, whereas feature-based entry may not be. Examples of this are numerous: Palm entering the smartphone category with its Treo device in the mid-2000s had some success in penetrating the market until Apple entered the fray leveraging iTunes and superior apps; Softsoap® was successful only because of the strategic control point of the pumps, not because of the liquid feature of the soap; new flavors or variants of existing packaged goods (for example, new bottles for cleaners or new flavors of yogurt) are quickly imitated by rivals; Internet connectivity of just about every device out there (locks, alarms, and security devices, home networks) is quickly imitated by rivals; the list goes on.

Key Points in Developing a Strategic Control Point

- The business of a strategic control point may or may not be profitable in its own right.
- Gaining control over the part of the value chain enabling strategic control enables greater value extraction at other points in the chain.
- Strategic control provides the basis for a sustainable competitive advantage in the value chain, that is, it cannot be temporary or fleeting unless the objective is short-run in nature (as in the Softsoap® example).
- There can be more than one strategic control point.
- It's often worth asking the question, "Could one of my competitors gain access to this strategic control point?" If the answer is yes, then it may be important from a defensive perspective.
- Is the investment commensurate with the rate of return? Sometimes, investing in a strategic control point can be prohibitive; therefore, it may not make sense to compete in this market. For example, in patent-protected markets, such as pharmaceuticals, chemicals, and medical devices, the R&D needed to work around existing patents is often prohibitively expensive, which can mean it makes little sense to enter until near the end of a patent expiry. The discipline required to make a decision of this sort is crucial to success.

Expanding along the Value Chain Follows a Classic Process

- Determine the long-run strategic vision and work back from your current core a step at a time.
- Map out the value chain in detail.
- Identify key strategic control points and areas for potential value extraction (in the Jeppesen Marine example, the control points

were data and bridge access and the sweet spot for value extraction in the channel was the fuel savings through VVOS).

- Map out core competencies across all players in the market across all areas of the value chain. We call this the competition and capabilities map.

- Assess organic versus inorganic competency acquisition for areas where competencies are lacking in key strategic control points. Acquisitions are generally preferred in areas where the "new math" applies, particularly in the case of speed to market, as was the case for Jeppesen in the digital marine navigation market.

- Map out the competitive landscape beyond your core market. Are there unexpected effects or new opportunities you might anticipate?

- You may find that core competencies in areas of strategic control and/or margin extraction are weak relative to key competitors in key markets. Additionally, you may discover that organic and inorganic competency acquisition is not feasible or financially realistic. These are cases that may warrant an exit plan or a no-entry decision. Make the tough decision. The art of the wise is in knowing what to overlook.

Chapter Summary and Key Business Principles

- Value chain analysis begins with the industry supply chain but then traces competition both horizontally and vertically.

- The business objective of value chain analysis is often to detect areas where advantageous margin opportunities exist and where strategic leverage may be exerted.

- Strategic control points exist where access to and control of that part of the value chain can result in substantial advantages throughout the value chain and in the market more broadly.

- Expanding along the value chain follows a classic process:
  - Determine the long-run strategic vision and work back from your current core a step at a time.
  - Map out the value chain in detail.
  - Identify key strategic control points and areas for potential value extraction.
  - Map out core competencies across all players in the market across all areas of the value chain.
  - For areas where competencies are lacking in key strategic control points, assess organic versus inorganic competency acquisition.
  - In markets where core competencies in areas of strategic control and/or margin extraction are weak relative to key competitors and where organic and inorganic competency acquisition is not feasible or financially realistic, an exit plan or a no-entry decision may be warranted. Make the tough decision.
- Matching areas of competency in key areas of the value chain can help guide strategic investment, particularly in areas where gaps may exist.

Key Business Tools

- Value chain analysis
- Strategic control points
- Competitive and capability maps

Targeting the Right Customers in the Right Space with the Right Offering

Pivot from strategy to tactics: strategic segmentation and value proposition—prioritization and following the money.

> —"Ruthlessly Prioritize"—sign in Sheryl Sandberg's conference room at Facebook headquarters.[1]

The Story of Henry Ford and the Vagabonds

Willie Sutton was a notorious bank robber. When asked why he robbed banks, incredulous, he responded, "Because that's where the money is."[2] If only companies would adopt the same single-minded obsession with following the money. We think of segmentation as many things; however, we should consider it first and foremost as a tool to strategically prioritize business opportunities, the commonly accepted business practice of following the money.

Inside of the value chain, segmentation is about prioritization above all else—as much about what to overlook as what to focus on.

To begin, we need to be clear about what segmentation is *not*— and if you read no further than this paragraph in this book, your time reading may have been well spent. Repeat after me: *you cannot segment products*. There is no getting around this as priority number one in segmentation; yet it is perhaps one of the most common mistakes, one of the most common "Rizzutoisms," in business.

You segment customers or customer needs, not products. Think of it this way: products (or more generally, offerings) are *what you deliver to customers in order to meet their needs*. You determine your customers' needs and then—based on the ones that offer the greatest margins, are growing the fastest, and so on—you deliver the offerings that satisfy the most attractive segments and spend development, R&D, and launch budgets in proportion to this attractiveness. Companies often segment products, which is an inside-out approach in that it's one that puts your organization's needs before the market's needs.

Segmentation is also crucial, since it is the point where you pivot from strategy to tactics. Once you have decided *where* to compete (via analysis of the value chain, strategic control points, and so on), your ability to prioritize and develop focused tactics (offering, price to extract value, points of access, and points of touch), including the value proposition for each segment, should follow logically. Indeed, one of the biggest mistakes companies make is to attempt to establish tactics before developing a thorough segmentation. How in the world can anyone determine what price to charge, how to access customers, what to say to them, and so forth, until they know *to whom* they're directing these efforts? If you are setting tactics without reference to appropriately constructed and prioritized segments, you are virtually flying blind. Firms do sometimes succeed this way, but, as the saying goes, "even the blind squirrel finds the nut sometimes."

This section will focus on how companies should approach segmentation, beginning with intuition and then taking us through process and theory. The intuition is simple and the process is straightforward, but actually doing it is hard work. It takes discipline and time. The alternative is a scattered approach to the market. Think of peppering a target with a shotgun rather than a series of well-focused laser guided rifle shots. While you may have some hits with the shotgun, I would much rather have a focused approach— one that homes in on important customers with laser beam precision, precisely the right message and exactly the right offering that produces the right result for you and for your customer. If you do this right, it forces rigid, obsessive prioritization. Good companies follow the money, making Willie Sutton proud.

Intuition

Imagine an annual camping trip with fireside conversations among Henry Ford, Thomas Edison, Harvey Firestone (as in Firestone Tire), and naturalist and author John Burroughs—spanning politics, economics, business, and other compelling issues of their time. Henry Ford is best known, of course, for the Ford Motor Company. However, perhaps one of his most interesting undertakings was with what has become known as the *Illustrious Vagabonds*. A camping trip with Henry Ford and Thomas Edison in 1914 was

Figure 5.1   The Illustrious Vagabonds.

Source: The collections of The Henry Ford.

the beginning of what became an annual event that grew in size, interest, and notoriety. In 1915, Ford and Edison were joined by Harvey Firestone and in 1916, by John Burroughs (who may have been the most famous of the four at the time). The four eventually became known as the Illustrious Vagabonds (source: HenryFord Estate.org) and formed the core of an annual camping expedition throughout the United States that grew to include a number of other participants (see Figure 5.1). What started as a modest trip turned into an annual media circus complete with photographer trucks, large-scale kitchen equipment, dining tables, and a caravan of accompanying vehicles. While early fireside chats between Ford and Edison never waned, we cannot overstate the interest and significance of what they meant to a burgeoning nation.

The story of the Illustrious Vagabonds fits perfectly in the context of this chapter, because it illustrates Henry Ford's ability to get past the clutter of the day and cut to the core—in this case, the core of an America thirsty for growth and exploration and its leaders' newfound wealth. We can think of Henry Ford's approach to segmentation. The now famous "You can have any color you want as long as it's black" was a euphemism for a standardized vehicle. It is what led Ford to famously determine that the Ford Motor Company would be successful if a common man—someone working on the floor of a Ford Motor Company factory—could afford one of his vehicles. Standardization lowered the cost sufficiently, and the average worker's productivity became high enough that someone working the factory floor could afford a shiny new Ford vehicle. Indeed, even Ford's choice of color mattered; it was black rather than any other color, because black paint dried the fastest.

The opposite of Ford's one-size-fits-all approach is one that's designed, built, and customized for the individual. The downside is that customization generally entails higher cost; the upside is that customers get *exactly* what they want. Examples of these abound nowadays: a bespoke suit from London's Savile Row or one custom-tailored in Hong Kong; a custom-designed and made dress; a custom-built house—all are current examples that are alive and well.[3]

The preferred approach—standardized as in Henry Ford or customized as in a Savile Row suit—depends upon the relative strength of the scale economies of standardization versus how well entrenched idiosyncratic preferences are at the individual level. If your customers don't have particularly strong preferences and scale economies are great (for example, televisions and most consumer electronics), a standardized approach is generally preferable. If, however, your customers have strong and heterogeneous preferences and scale economies are small or non-existent (for example, real estate services or any offering that requires customized service), a personalized approach would be preferable.

This is essentially the "global-local" debate that has gone on for the past couple of decades. The more idiosyncratic and different individual local preferences are, the better a local approach would work; alternatively, greater scale economies would encourage a global, standardized approach.[4] The issues in a global environment are fundamentally no different than the segmentation issues we address in this chapter.

Segmentation is intended to provide the best of both worlds—the cost efficiencies of the Henry Ford approach and the customized delivery of nearly bespoke items. If there are certain groups of customers with essentially the same (or similar) needs, why would you want to deliver bespoke, custom-designed offerings for *each* of them? Why not produce one offering that comes very close to each of their needs but takes advantage of the scale economies of the Henry Ford approach? Time Warner and other cable companies have a standard set of offerings across the United States, for example, but their delivery is customized for detailed segments—apartment dwellers get a different package than people living in single family homes; automobile companies are masters at this, with a lineup of vehicles that work off of a common platform but have variants tailored to each consumer segment. The result is the efficiency gains of scale economies and tailored offerings for each group. Further, grouping customers based on needs makes it possible to tailor the delivery for each group and then *prioritize* the groups so that you spend your time, resources, effort, and so on, on the most fruitful segments (whatever your criteria might be—more on this in a bit).

Two examples typify key elements of strategic segmentation: Nike illustrates how you get to key segments using something we call "beachheads," and American Express illustrates how and why you choose the segments in the first place—and, most important, highlights the consequences of choosing these segments.

Nike's Beachhead Strategies—Getting to the Key Segments and Following the Money

Nike exemplifies the notion of having a single-minded obsession with following the money. To see exactly how it does so, we look back and contrast Nike's beginnings versus rival Reebok's.[5]

In its early days, the cofounders of a company by the name of Blue Ribbon Sports began selling athletic shoes out of a car trunk. In what is now a legendary story, Phil Knight and his college track coach Bill Bowerman worked college campuses and the pockets of premier athletes at training facilities throughout North America. They eventually merged the company's focal brand, Nike (with the famous "swoosh" created in 1971 and the waffle soles that Bowerman invented using his wife's waffle iron), into Blue Ribbon Sports to form Nike, Inc., in 1978.[6]

One of the locations that they visited was the University of Alberta in Edmonton, Canada, the home of a group of premier athletes training for the Olympics at the time. Training at the University of Alberta was a young skater who went on to become Canadian national champion and a member of the national team from 1973 to 1980. The first time he saw a pair of Nike athletic shoes was one evening after a long day's training.

Back then, training would typically start at 6:00 AM when the gym doors opened. They'd take a break for the 9-to-5 job that paid the bills and then resumed training until the doors closed at 10:00 PM. Usually, the time between 9:30 and 10:00 PM featured athletes at various stages of showering and getting dressed after a hard day's training. One day, one of the athletes noticed a number of guys circled around a single male athlete. (For any of you that have ever spent time in a men's locker room, you know this is not a common sight!) The athletes were all laughing when they saw what the guy in the middle was holding up: a pair of Nikes that he'd pulled out of a canvas drawstring bag. What was so different about this pair of Nikes that had them all laughing?

The shoes that Nike produced differed from their main competitors at the time on two principal dimensions: first, they had the waffle sole with the wedge heel. This was meant to address the constant pounding that runners who cover many miles take—and the stress fractures, shin splints, and other ailments that running long distances can inflict on the body. Second, they were made from a synthetic nylon (allowing for funky colors) and not out of leather (such as shoes from Adidas, Puma, Tiger, and other competitors) or canvas (as in Converse). These features allowed them to breathe and be lighter on the feet. However, they looked flimsy and cheap at first glance. The other athletes couldn't believe that this athlete was going to entrust his feet—and his Olympic hopes—to this flimsy shoe that they assumed would allow his legs to be pounded into oblivion.

To make a long story short, the other athletes saw this athlete out on the track some time later. Much to their surprise, he still had these funny looking shoes on his feet. They pulled him aside and asked how many pairs he'd been through by that point. His response astounded them; this was still the original pair! He went on to extol the virtues of the shoe: they didn't get ruined in the rain, they were light on his feet, they breathed, they still had bounce to take the pounding due to the sole and the heel. This group of premier athletes was soon hooked, with every single one of them wearing these funny-looking shoes on their feet.

However, Nike isn't stupid. It remembered the Willie Sutton rule of following the money. Nike knew that the money wasn't with premier athletes; it was with the mass market. The athletes were a beachhead to get to the masses—and they hit it big with a long-distance runner by the name of Lasse Viren.

Viren famously won the long-distance double at the 1976 Olympics in Montreal, proceeding to take of his shoes—emblazoned with the Nike swoosh—and put them on his hands as he paraded around Olympic Stadium with all the world watching. Every evening newscast and broadcast throughout the world showed Lasse Viren celebrating his historic feat with the pair of funny-looking shoes on his hands. As a result, every amateur athlete around the world wanted these funny-looking shoes on his or her feet (not hands)!

And so, Nike was born.

They followed a similar beachhead strategy with Michael Jordan in basketball and Tiger Woods in golf, knowing at every turn where the money was.

In order to fully understand Nike's power of execution, we contrast its approach with that of Reebok, a company that was even more successful with its beachhead—and was almost destroyed by it. Some of you might recall that Reebok's original beachhead was women's aerobics. In fact, Reebok became so successful in women's aerobics that it became almost a uniform for the sport (remember "Step Reebok"?).

So what was wrong with this beachhead?

Not only did it wall off half the market (males), it effectively excluded everyone outside of its original beachhead. If you're 16 or 17 years old, male *or* female, *the last thing you want to be caught dead wearing* are the shoes that your mother wears to her aerobics class. Reebok's choice of beachhead created a *barrier* rather than a bridge between its original target market and the mass market. Reebok found the beachhead and lost sight of the money.

What is the beachhead for your market—the path or customer group that will lead you *to* the money and the market's sweet spot? Think carefully about this one, because finding a successful beachhead is not enough. Finding one that gives you entrée to the right segments is the key; just ask Reebok!

American Express and the Strategic Implications of Segmentation Choice

Have you ever lost a credit card? Was it a MasterCard? Visa? Discover? American Express? How long did it take you to replace it? Ever wonder about why it took so long—or didn't? Ever think about who is winning the credit card wars today? What metrics would you use to determine the answer to this?

In order to answer these questions, it might be illustrative to go back to the very beginning of the industry—before ATMs and Internet banking, when all we knew were cash and savings and checking accounts and, yes, Travelers Cheques.

Not many people know what the first credit card was or the year it was issued—there is an interesting story here. In 1949, Frank McNamara, head of the Hamilton Credit Corporation, went out to eat with Alfred Bloomingdale, McNamara's long-time friend and grandson of the founder of Bloomingdale's department store, and McNamara's attorney Ralph Sneider. The three men were eating at Major's Cabin Grill, a famous New York restaurant located next to the Empire State Building, and discussing a problem customer of the Hamilton Credit Corporation.

At the end of the meal with his two friends, McNamara reached into his pocket for his wallet so that he could pay for the meal (in cash). He was shocked to discover that he had forgotten his wallet. To his embarrassment, he then had to call his wife and have her bring him some money. McNamara vowed never to let this happen again.

Motivated by this, they came up with a new idea, a form of payment—a credit card—that customers could use at multiple locations. What was particularly novel about this concept was that there would be a middleman between companies and their customers (as opposed to store cards that were issued by the store and had no middleman). McNamara discussed the idea with Bloomingdale and Sneider, and the three pooled some money and started a new company in 1950, which they called Diners Club.

It was a novel business model at the time. Instead of individual merchants offering credit to their own customers (as they often did at that time, billing them later), Diners Club was going to offer credit to individuals for many companies and bill the customers in turn.

In order to make a profit without charging interest (interest-bearing credit cards came much later), the companies that accepted the Diners Club credit card were charged 7 percent for each transaction, while the subscribers to the credit card had to pay a $3 annual fee.

McNamara's new credit company focused on salesmen, since these were the people who often needed to dine (hence the new company's name) at multiple restaurants to entertain their clients. Therefore, Diners Club needed to both convince a large number of restaurants to accept the new card and to get salesmen to subscribe. The first Diners Club credit cards were issued in 1950 to 200 people (most were friends and acquaintances of McNamara) and accepted by 14 restaurants in New York.

In the beginning, progress was slow. Merchants didn't want to pay the Diners Club fee and didn't want competition for their own store cards; customers didn't want to sign up unless there were a large number of merchants that accepted the card. However, the popularity of the card grew and by the end of 1950, 20,000 people were using the Diners Club credit card.[7]

An ancillary motivation for credit cards was related to the advent of valet parking in Europe in the 1800s. In much the same way that valet parking kept you safe from the London and Paris thieves in the alleys between where you parked your carriage and the fancy restaurant, Diners Club kept your cash safe as you went to a participating restaurant.

Fast forward to today: who would you say is currently winning the credit card battle? Diners Club? Probably not. American Express? MasterCard? Visa? What metrics would you use to determine the answer? You might suggest measures such as margins, number of customers, overall profitability, delinquency rates, and/or revenue per customer or card. Let's take a look at some of these by using some recent numbers (2011, U.S. only) and examining key indicators, recognizing that these are just a few of many metrics that may be used to assess the relative success of each card (we use these in large part due to the accessibility of the largely proprietary nature of the data).[8]

Upon examining the relatively simple numbers in Figure 5.2, it looks pretty good for MasterCard and Visa. The combined revenue run through MasterCard and Visa (almost $1.4 trillion) versus American Express ($540 billion) and over four times as many transactions indicates that MasterCard and Visa dominate. However, taking a deeper look into the revenue and incremental

	American Express	Visa	MasterCard
Number of Cards in Circulation	50.6 million	234.1 million	175.7 million
Number of Transactions	3.8 billion	10.39 billion	6.1 billion
Annual $ Charged	$540 billion	$888 billion	$508 billion
Annual $ spend per card member	$ 10,671	$3,793	$2,891

Figure 5.2   The Credit Card Wars of Today.

contribution per transaction tells a very different story. As you can see in Figures 5.3 and Figure 5.4, American Express has a huge advantage both in terms of revenue per transaction and in terms of contribution per each transaction.

American Express clearly dominates in terms of revenue per transaction and effective margin per transaction. Further, it is not just the average revenue per transaction metric that is interesting. The 2012 third-quarter credit card delinquency rate report also shows that there is merit in the customer segment that American Express focuses on: its delinquency rate is just 1.31 percent versus 2.44 percent for Citibank, 3.16 percent for Capital One and 3.23 percent for Bank of America.

	American Express	Visa	MasterCard
Average Spend Per Transaction	$142	$85	$83
Exchange Fees	2.54%	1.8%	1.75%
Average Revenue Per Transaction	$3.61	$1.53	$1.45

Figure 5.3   Some Metrics of Success—American Express, Visa, and MasterCard.

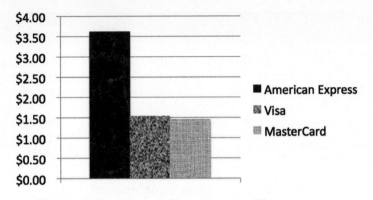

Figure 5.4   Average Revenue per Transaction.

Think back to the early days of American Express. The founders had a choice of segments to go after: two of many possible choices were a focused niche strategy (which is what they chose) or a mass-market strategy (one that was left to Visa and MasterCard). In the end, American Express clearly chose the segments that it did because of their profitability. However, people often miss the operational implications of segment choice. Given the niche strategy of the high-revenue, high-margin customers that American Express focuses on, the company must support its offering with a high level of service and support. By contrast, Visa and MasterCard's mass-market strategy cannot afford to deliver similar levels of service and support. Thus, while choice of segments is important for the customers that you target, it also has implications for what you deliver; after all, you need the core competencies to be able to deliver them!

There are two main lessons to be taken from the numbers in this example:

1. *Choice of segments*. American Express had the nascent market at its feet. It could have gone for any segment it wanted, but it

chose the segments with high margins (airline tickets, hotel rooms, client dinners), where it could provide a competitive advantage with a barrier to entry. The company already had a network infrastructure in place—a global network of Travel Related Services (TRS) establishments (read Travelers Cheques) that allowed it to provide superior service throughout the world. A potential competitor, on the other hand, would have to establish a network from scratch in order to serve this high-end clientele as well. American Express focused on high-margin customers where there were significant barriers to entry— an ideal choice of segments in any young, growing industry.

2. *Operational implications of segment choice.* We often fail to think about the operational implications of the segments that we choose; think about what the choice of segments did for American Express, MasterCard, and Visa. The last two, whose cards are aimed at the mass market, need to focus on two things: get volume up and costs down. If it cost Mastercard $1.75 per transaction, the $1.45 per transaction in revenue won't keep them in business for very long; the old tongue-in-cheek saying "we lose money on every unit, but make it up in volume" applies here. So, they needed to invest in building operational capabilities and lowering costs while simultaneously spending on advertising to get volume up given the small per-transaction margins.

By contrast, American Express needs to justify the contribution per transaction and the relatively high merchant fees. Want an airline ticket or a reservation at the hottest restaurant in town? Call American Express Business Platinum Concierge. If an American Express machine goes down at a retailer, the company services it quickly. Ever lose a credit card? I've lost two. One was a MasterCard that I lost while on holiday in Barcelona. When I reported it, the customer service representative said "Don't worry, we'll send it out tomorrow on overnight delivery." But I was in Barcelona and hence the dreaded, albeit inevitable response: "I'm sorry, but for security reasons, we can't send it anywhere but to your home address." When I lost my American Express card back in 1995, I was living in Sydney, Australia. I got home to Kirribilli (across Sydney Harbor from the Opera House) about 10:00 PM and reported it lost at 10:00 AM the next morning. I was told that I could come to the Pitt Street branch after 2:00 PM that same day to get my new card—just four hours later! So, I took the ferry to Circular Quay and had my card in hand that afternoon.

Service, an existing network, and an advantage for customers willing to pay for it—this is segmentation at its best. Prioritization. Follow the money; Willie Sutton would have been proud.

Top 10 Segmentation Rizzutoisms (with apologies to David Letterman)

1. Segmenting based on product (inside out).
2. Not "segmenting down" into market.
3. Not exploring multiple bases.
4. Using segments that are not practically useful.
5. Segmentation that is unduly complicated.
6. Shelving good analysis.
7. Not tying value propositions to segments.
8. Not integrating back to front in organization.
9. Failing to appropriately prioritize.
10. Overspending on consultants.

Given the appropriate priorities, where do you begin? This is a common question asked by managers in the field. Consequently, we begin by examining the process of segmentation.

Process

As a manager, what do you need to know in order to facilitate, lead, and critique segmentation efforts? Below is a list of key things to do in order to ensure a useful, productive, and pragmatic segmentation effort:

1. Always look to the customer needs and attributes first; this is rule No. 1 when it comes to segmentation.

2. Push hard on alternative segmentation schemes—and make sure they stick. Like you'll see in the SAS example that follows, truly innovative approaches generally only come after people are forced to think differently.

3. Ensure that teams segment down into the market. If you see a segmentation effort that consists of only one layer (for example, a region or gender or industry type), it is almost certainly not deep enough—so push back hard.

4. Make sure that creative efforts have been attempted. Don't let a team present one answer as if it were "Manna from Heaven"; make sure that the group has explored multiple bases for segmentation and numerous creative avenues, that is, those that they haven't explored before.

5. Test a group's homogeneity on key segmentation elements. This is the crucial part of ensuring you have a valid segment; the needs in each should be homogeneous.

6. Break with research in between initial and secondary efforts; this allows an unbiased team to gather data accurately.

7. Make sure segmentation is actionable. Avoid choosing segments that may make sense but can't be practically implemented on the ground.

8. Acid test with segment evaluation table. This enables you to appropriately prioritize the segments you envision and may be the key to success.

9. Write value propositions that are based directly on segmentation efforts. If you have written a value proposition before nailing down your segmentation, you'll only get this right through chance.

10. Set priorities and weights up front—get your team to agree on this early, since it's critical to getting buy-in at the end of the process.

The process of segmentation is outlined here and designed for a firm in a B2B setting—one where there is a deep and intimate knowledge of the customer. Typically, the front end of the process will be different in a B2C setting; we take different steps when we have 240 million customers (for example, for a new soft drink or a new brand of cereal) than when we have, say, 140 major clients (for example, for the Boeing Company). But, regardless of whether we are segmenting a B2B or a B2C market, the intuition is the same. Hence, while we may use surveys and clustering algorithms in a large B2C setting, the essence of what we do is fundamentally similar to the process described here. Only the details will vary.

Process of Segmentation

Step 1: Choose segment selection criteria and weights.

Step 2: Categorize customers or customer needs into homogeneous groups.

Step 3: Iterate over and over. And over again. And again.

Step 4: Determine customer needs (attribute weights) by segment.

Step 5: Prioritize across segments.

Step 6: Write value proposition for key segments.

Step 7: Organizationally implement segmentation scheme.

Step 8: Revise, revisit, and revise again.

How-to Guide for Managers

Imagine it's Wednesday about 11:20 AM. You've been part of an eight-person senior leadership team locked in a room since 8 AM on Monday morning. You are working a segmentation strategy session and have hit a wall. You've tried every imaginable creative way to approach and segment your customers, and the consultant facilitating these sessions has told you that you can't leave the room—under the threat of no lunch—until you are able to develop a new and innovative approach (basis) to segmentation. Do you walk out and fire the consultant? Do you keep pushing on?

This was exactly the situation I faced a few years back when working with the senior leadership team of SAS, the largest privately held software company in the world. To their credit, they didn't fire me; they stuck with it. About 11:50 AM, one senior executive said, "What if we think about it this way . . ." and they were off. By 12:30 PM, I couldn't get them to leave the room. The strategy that came out of those sessions resulted in a successful launch in the market the following year, all borne out of pushing the boundaries via the methodology described next. Following the process flow and trusting the process is crucial.

Segmentation Exercise

There are two overarching principles important in segmenting a market. The first is to divide the market into its separate homogeneous submarkets (segments). The second step is to select which segments the firm should target (which are most attractive). You can then use this information to write a winning value proposition.

This exercise will also allow you to gain additional perspective on your customers with the aim of achieving a greater level of strategic and organizational agility.

(continued)

(*continued*)

1. Dividing the market into its segments—big picture

   a. Defining the attributes

   Let's start at the 30,000-foot level, by picking one area of a market that's of interest to your company. For all of the customers in the market (potential and current), list the attributes that you feel are important to them when they're selecting their supplier. For example, one might specify the following attributes in selecting a personal laptop computer:

   1. Processing speed

   2. Brand name

   3. Price

   4. Size of screen

   5. Hard drive capacity

   6. Connectivity (USB, Bluetooth, etc.)

   7. Distribution channel (where you buy it)

   Of course, not everyone in this market is interested in the same thing. Some customers may be interested in finding a low price while others are concerned with getting the highest overall performance. The different groups of customers interested in different attributes are the segments (novices may be interested in a low price and easy-to-use features, whereas experienced gamers may be interested in fast graphics processing and large storage capacity).

   Next, list these attributes for the part of the market where you're focusing on a board or flip chart.

   b. Defining the segments

   Now, use "tree" diagrams (see the detailed discussion below) to segment your customers or constituent groups into sections where needs are similar within the group but different across groups. For example, in the computer scenario, we may begin by segmenting those on a Windows or Mac operating system, then divide each of those groups into "techies" who may want high computing power and average users, corporate versus individual purchases, laptop (mobile) versus desktop (stationary) needs, and so on. In specifying the segments, be sure to specify the *basis* for segmenting the market. Can you segment down into the market beyond the initial cut?

c. Putting it all together

Use the columns in Table 5.1 to specify the segments that exist in your market that you have just come up with (feel free to choose more or fewer than four; in practice, we would have many). Then, specify how important each attribute is to each segment (ideally, we can use input from a choice/conjoint analysis described below).

One way to test whether you've segmented correctly is to see if the segments truly are different, that is, that each segment requires a distinct marketing mix. Does each of the columns have a unique set of attribute priorities? If they do not, you'll need to revisit Table 5.1 to see if there is a

Table 5.1

Segments	A	B	C	D
Attributes				
1.				
2.				
3.				
4.				
5.				
6.				
7.				

(continued)

(*continued*)

different way the market should be segmented that would yield submarkets with greater differences.

2. Segment selection

Once you've segmented your market, it is necessary to decide specifically where you should focus your attention. Those who want to sell or spend their time with everyone are generally suffering from a lack of focus. Electing to focus on multiple segments usually requires a different approach.

The segment selection is usually based on the attractiveness of the segments and the firm's ability to appeal to the segment. The first element can be based on several factors such as segment size (volume), growth rate, concentration of customers, margins, the cost to serve, and so on.

You want to evaluate each of the segments identified in Table 5.1 on the attractiveness criterion you have specified in

Table 5.2

Segments	A	B	C	D
Attractiveness				
Criterion				
1. Market size				
2. Growth rate				
3. Sustainability				
4. Margins				
5. Cost to serve				
6. Strategic fit				
Total Attractiveness				

the first column where 1 is very unattractive and 10 is very attractive. Can you think of ways to put a range or a distribution on each score (perhaps using simulations or "Monte Carlo" techniques)? How might you use this approach to hedge risk? Are these generic criteria the ones that you would want to use for your market?

Finally, based on the data you've inserted in Table 5.2, what are your primary and secondary targets? Are they the same today as they would be in 5 years? In 10 years? Does this suggest opportunities for working with outside organizations to develop new capabilities?

Building on this SAS example, a process flow for a session with your team might include the following steps.

I. Segmentation
   1. Day one: begin with customer needs analysis.
   2. Determine segmentation attractiveness criteria and weights.
   3. Work through tree diagrams and alternative bases for segmentation.
   4. Rip up efforts and start again. Over. And over. And over again.
   5. Select two to three ideas that provide insight for further investigation.
   6. Compare with prior efforts and traditional approaches.

II. Attribute and segment prioritization tables—research
   7. Take two to four weeks into the future to let research gather relevant data.
   8. Review customer attribute table and segment priorities.

III. Segment prioritization and value proposition for key segments

9. Prioritize segments, develop value proposition and overall tactics.

10. Develop detailed value proposition for key segments following from the analysis.

Let's examine each step in a bit more detail:

I. Segmentation

The very first thing to do when working with an organization is to get the team in your customers' mind-set. The first exercise is to have team members list customers and spend time brainstorming their needs, broadly defined. You won't use this later, at least not in any formal capacity. But since a successful segmentation exercise requires that you see the market as the customer does, this process emphasizes the paramount need for customer focus. This is one of the toughest things for those operating in the technical and scientific space to grasp.

The second thing to do is to set segment criteria and weights. Think back to the example from the introduction and ask yourself: How many times have you sat in a meeting where the conversation goes something like the one set up in the introduction?

Joe: "I think segment A should be our No. 1 priority; the growth rates are insane."

Harry: "No, the margins on segment B are through the roof; we should focus on B."

Sue: "You've both missed the point. Segment C is by far the largest and has been our major customer for 20 years now."

As noted earlier, who typically wins these matches? Usually it's the person who yells the loudest; or, more often, the one with the highest position in the organizational chart. Who do you *want* to win? The one who is right, of course. By setting out the criteria for what would make one segment more attractive than another before undergoing the exercise, you ensure a more objective, fair evaluation of each segment's attractiveness. You ultimately want to win with the best segments for the business objectives at hand with the right prioritization.

In practice, groups should determine what would make one segment more attractive than another. Typical standard criteria are things like growth rates, margins, competitive pressures, size of market, strategic fit, and so on. These criteria could be numerous, and the weights used can be complicated to set. To their credit, the senior leadership team at John Deere (in the Consumer and Commercial Equipment division at the time) approached this correctly. When they were taking riding lawn equipment to big box store such as Lowes and Home Depot, they took a full day to discuss, debate, and arrive at a final set of criteria and appropriate set of weights for what would make one segment more attractive than another. They recognized the importance of setting such parameters. In doing so, though, be sure you don't inadvertently overweigh certain criteria. It's easy to give high weights to margin, segment profits, and relative market size when they're related to the same underlying construct—strategic control in the value chain—and you're triple-counting the same construct as a result. Be sure you do this up front and engender buy-in from the teams. When each team member helps construct the weights, it's difficult for any one of them to criticize the outcome!

The critical part of the process is the segmentation effort itself. Recall that the objective is to divide the market into groups where the needs are similar within each group, but different across the groups. This allows you to generate directed tactics for each group and set appropriate prioritization of resources among and across them. This is why dividing the diverse set of customer needs into homogeneous groups is perhaps the most important step. While companies in a B2C market with numerous customers typically complete this step via survey and methodological tools,[9] it's preferable to use a more subjective, albeit more ad hoc, approach. This allows you to take advantage of managers' detailed knowledge of markets and customers.

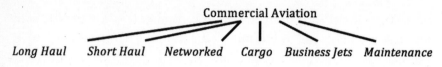

Figure 5.5 Commercial Aviation.

To demonstrate, imagine you are leading an effort to segment the needs of customers of the world's 140 major airlines, from American Airlines to Virgin. One logical way to group needs of commercial aviation customers is shown in Figure 5.5.

Clearly, those operating on a short-haul route (Southwest in the United States or Ryanair in Europe, for example) have different needs from transatlantic customers, who in turn have different needs from those carrying cargo (FedEx, UPS, and DHL, for example). Are any of the categories above segments? No. Needs are nowhere near homogeneous in these groups. For example, we can segment down into the market for each of the high-level segments (long haul, short haul, networked carriers, cargo, business jets, and maintenance).

Let's examine the short-haul group in more detail and ask: How do some short-haul carriers' needs differ from others? One answer might have to do with regional differences; those traveling in Asia need galleys on board to serve hot meals on even short flights. In the United States, we have small galleys and different seat configurations, whereas in Europe, companies like Ryanair have lobbied to allow passengers to stand while strapped to a board! So, we might sub-segment the short-haul group as in Figure 5.6.

Looking at the North American short-haul segment, as an example, we once again ask the question: "Do customers in this group have relatively homogeneous needs?" Again, the answer is no.

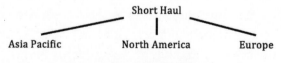

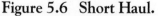

Figure 5.6 Short Haul.

Southwest, which utilizes a low-cost carrier (LCC) model, has different needs from a full-fare differentiator (FFD) model (for example, Alaskan Air). Once we've gotten to the segment of LCC operators on short-haul routes in North America, the needs are reasonably homogeneous. At this point, we have a segment, and should continue this process through every branch.

Now, you may be asking, "Where do you stop?" You can't keep going until you have a single customer and a single application; that wouldn't be very useful. There's an old adage that says "there is a segment in every market, but not necessarily a market in every segment." The answer is that you do indeed just need to keep going. There is a litmus test you can use to tell if you've gone too far and gotten too granular (we'll get to that in a minute).

Now tear it up. Again. *And again. And, yes, once again.* Yes, I just told you to destroy all your hard work over and over again. Let me elaborate.

Let's come back to that SAS example. I typically have a group run through the exercise we just discussed and present in front of a room on a flip chart. Then, when they have finished presenting, I dramatically tear up the paper from the flip chart with all of their hard work on it into little pieces at the front of the room. Then I tell them that they need to do it again. Only, this time, they can't use any of the criteria (short haul, long haul, or region or LCC business model) that they have previously used; they have to use *different* criteria. They then go back and work hard, only to present and have me tear it up once again. And again. And again. Until they get stuck. Like what happened with the SAS team.

Think of it this way. Invariably, the first few efforts—the ones that come relatively easily—are business as usual. Long haul, short haul, region, business model; these are not particularly insightful. It's when you get *stuck* that the valuable insights come. Some examples may be how airlines use information to interconnect (see Chapter 7 on vertical alignment) or their technological progressiveness, cash position, wage structure, fleet age, or a whole host of other ways of grouping their needs together that haven't been thought of before. It's all done in an attempt to gain new insight into delivering offerings that better meet customer needs. It's actually hard work and takes time, but companies that do it well generally succeed.

II. Attribute and segment prioritization tables—research

Okay, so imagine you've done a dozen of these and truly *have* exhausted the set of possibilities. What now? You should pick out two or three of these for their insight; often the standard way of approaching markets is included as a benchmark. Then walk away— at least for a few weeks.

Parallel teams must then research these key segments, investigating the crucial information that's needed before teams can reassemble to assess strategic implications. But even before that can happen, you must determine what information you need to turn the segmentation work to date into an executable strategy. This requires you to focus on two objectives: (1) detailing the segments' attribute needs and (2) prioritizing the segments using the criteria developed earlier. It's essential to give this research to independent teams, as this ensures that there won't be any bias in the numbers that they come up with.

You need to collect two main sets of information for each of the segment schemes derived (represented here in table form): (1) attribute needs by segment and (2) segment prioritization data (which correspond to the two objectives above). Think of these in terms of the following two tables that a research team can complete to support the segmentation effort.

Let's focus on four segments from the earlier example: short-haul North America LCC model (A); short-haul North America FFD model (B); short-haul Europe, LCC model (C); and short-haul Europe FFD model (D). Imagine that we had conducted a choice analysis (covered in the next chapter), and that customers in these segments rated the four key attributes—Cost per Available Seat Mile or CASM, cargo capacity, the sophistication of the in-flight entertainment system (IFE), and final delivered price—in terms of importance on a scale of 1 to 10 (10 being most important in the purchase decision, 1 not at all important):

Segments	A	B	C	D
Attributes				
1. CASM	10	10	10	10
2. Cargo	9	9	3	9
3. IFE	5	5	7	2
4. Price	8	8	2	7

A few things stand out from this table.

1. *A litmus test.* Segments A and B are the same. This is the litmus test referenced earlier that indicates that we should not have continued this far in the earlier segmentation exercise. Therefore, we can combine them into a single segment.
2. *Must-have attributes.* Cost per available seat mile is clearly one of these, as it's a focal point for customer decisions.
3. *Segmentation opportunities.* Only three out of the four segments are overly price sensitive, and segment C may be interested in paying more if the IFE and CASM are right. This warrants further study.

The second thing for the research team to do at this time is to conduct a segmentation prioritization study. They can use the criteria and weights established earlier to independently evaluate each segment in terms of its size, margins, growth, competition, and so forth. From this, you can derive segment scores (and even place potential distributions on the estimates, run Monte Carlo simulations, and so on) and develop prioritization for each of the segmentation schemes developed. Ultimately, you can determine which one of these to use in practice based on the strategic opportunities that present themselves after all of this analysis; in part, it's simply a judgment call.

III. Segment prioritization and value proposition for key segments

Finally, after the research teams complete this analysis, the strategy teams reconvene. Armed with this information, you can establish priorities across the segments and begin to implement a detailed tactical plan. Part of this plan will be the value proposition defined as follows:

> A *value proposition is the promise you make to the targeted segments, one that resonates with the key attributes for that segment (fill in the blanks)*:
> *For* TARGET SEGMENT X, *the* YOUR PRODUCT OR SERVICE *provides* KEY BENEFITS *[in the customer's mind that they care about] and is better than the competition because of* KEY SALIENT DIFFERENTIATOR ATTRIBUTES.

Think about the earlier example. Imagine the segment evaluation had led you to target segment D (short-haul Europe FFD model) and that you were competitive on CASM but had a strategic advantage of superior cargo capacity. In this case, the value proposition for this segment (yes—you need one for each segment and must make sure they are consistent) for the imaginary HondaJet Enterprise 900 is straightforward:

> For *differentiator airlines operating short-haul European routes, the HondaJet Enterprise 900 provides best-in-class cost-per-available-seat-mile at a competitive delivered price and is better than competitors in this class due to its superior cargo capacity.*

Think about what you've derived from this process. The value proposition homes in on the key attributes that the customers in this segment care about and focuses on your strategic competitive advantage (if it doesn't, you need to go back to the R&D or acquisition drawing board). Additionally, the process has led you to appropriately prioritize these segments in terms of your efforts, time, budget, resources, and so on. You deliver the offering to the most important segments with offerings and customer value propositions that resonate with them precisely because *they were developed for them*. Companies like Nike are flawless in their execution of these principles and have been largely successful as a result.

It bears repeating here: good companies have a single-minded obsession with following the money. The prioritization that results from this segmentation process is one that would have made Willie Sutton proud.

Finally, it is important to emphasize once again that the intuition for the process is identical in B2C markets. However, the tree diagrams noted above simply won't work with the large number of customers that are typical for a B2C application. The use of large-scale surveys, clustering techniques, and mathematical analysis of correlations are considerably more common (what the trees do above, analysis of correlations across subjects does in a large-scale consumer setting), and generally more appropriate in these situations. However, the ad hoc method of relying on correlations fails to utilize the valuable insights managers bring to bear on the problem when they work a segmentation effort in real time. So use this experience in your markets; invariably, there is a wealth of knowledge that can provide insights that an analysis of correlations will almost always miss.

Chapter Summary and Key Business Principles

- You can't segment products, only customers and customer needs.
- The biggest Rizzutoism imaginable is not failing to segment down into the market.
- Think beyond standard demographic, standard industrial classification (SIC), gender, socioeconomic status, and psychographic bases.

- You must adhere to the process rigorously; it's hard work.
- Segmenting a B2B market follows same principles as a B2C market, but with significant differences in process and inputs.
- Good segmentation analysis is key to appropriate tactics and is the building block of a good marketing strategy.
- Follow the process closely:
  - Segment the market multiple ways. Get stuck.
  - Produce attribute tables for the segments. Validate that you haven't gone too far.
  - Prioritize through the use of segment prioritization tables.
  - Focus on key segments as you plan moving forward. Prioritize.
  - Value proposition statement should be written for high-priority segments and should follow closely the attribute table above along with competitive gap analysis.
  - Tactics should focus on segment-specific needs and positioning.

Some General Rules to Remember

- Localized, strong, idiosyncratic preferences and small economies of scale favor customized offerings tailored to the individual.
- Strong scale economies and relatively weak individual preferences favor standardized offerings.
- In reality, we are invariably in between the two extremes—segmentation is the process that allows us to bridge the gap and prioritize appropriately.

Key Business Tools

- Market segmentation process
- Segment evaluation and prioritization criteria

- Tree diagrams and segment groupings via segmenting down into the market via multiple bases
- Attribute tables and segment validation
- Segment prioritization
- Value proposition

Exercise: Is Kindle Fire Stealing Market Share from iPad?

When Amazon launched Kindle Fire in the autumn of 2011, many industry analysts predicted that it would take market share from Apple's iPad. But based on data published by market research firm IDC in 2012, this is simply not the case. Why is that?

Now that you understand how market segmentation works, let's practice. Answer the following questions:

- How many segments are there in the tablet market? Remember to segment deep down into the market—the deeper, the better. Use the tree diagram.
- What are the different segments' needs for the tablet? Are these segments indeed different segments?
- What is the price sensitivity of each?
- What are their attribute needs/salient differentiators that drive purchases?
- Which segment does the iPad fit?
- Which segment does the Kindle Fire fit?

Once you have gone through this exercise, it will be easy to see that iPad and Kindle Fire are indeed products for two different segments of the market. The iPad is in a league of its

(continued)

(*continued*)

own, whereas the Kindle Fire is competing in the rest of the market segments where price sensitivity is a big deal. It might take the lion's share of the *rest* of the market.

Top Five Vendors, Worldwide Media Tablet Shipments, Second Quarter 2012 (Preliminary) (unit shipments are in thousands)[10]

Vendor	2Q12 Shipments	Market Share	2Q11 Shipments	Market Share	2Q12/ 2Q11 Growth
1. Apple	17,042	68.2%	9,248	61.5%	84.3%
2. Samsung	2,391	9.6%	1,099	7.3%	117.6%
3. Amazon. com	1,252	5.0%	0	NA	NA
4. ASUS	855	3.4%	397	2.6%	115.5%
5. Acer	385	1.5%	629	4.2%	−38.7%
Others	3,067	12.3%	3,668	24.4%	−16.4%
All Vendors	24,994	100%	15,042	100%	66.2%

Understanding Your Customers in the Right Space

The Use of Choice Theory and Customer Choice Analytics
—The Story of the Coke and the Temperature Sensitive
Vending Machine[1]

T his chapter kicks off with an exercise. You are tasked with discerning what the following eight management decisions have in common:

Decision 1: Framing. It's a hot summer day; temperatures are running in the high 90s with searing humidity. You've been running around in the scorching heat and develop a strong thirst. You spot a vending machine and gratefully make your way over to it. The price of a can of Coke posted on the vending machine is $1.25. However, there is a sign that states, "If the outside temperature is above 90 degrees Fahrenheit, then the price will be raised to $1.75." Do you feel taken advantage of when you have to pay $1.75 rather than $1.25 because it's so hot outside? Seventy-seven percent of respondents in recent experiments did; they objected to such a pricing system and felt "gouged" and taken advantage of.

Now, imagine the following. You walk up to that same vending machine and the posted price is $1.75, but the sign now states, "If the outside temperature is below 90 degrees Fahrenheit, then the price will be reduced to $1.25." Do you no longer feel taken advantage of? Interestingly, a full 78 percent of respondents *didn't* mind this pricing system even though it is the same *exact* pricing system as the first. It's just *framed* differently! It's the same price conveyed two different ways, yet we get polar opposite responses on the part of actual customers.

Decision 2: Setting list price. You are a lawn equipment manufacturer and need to set prices in advance of the crucial upcoming spring selling season. You know the way that your customers react to your price list will depend upon what prices your rivals set, and you don't know yet what these

117

prices will be. Do you wait and let your competitors set prices first? Do you set your prices and then adjust in reaction to your competitors' prices once they are set? Do you set yours independent of your rivals' pricing and hope for the best, selling off inventory at the end of the season at substantially reduced prices if need be?

Decision 3: Avoiding a price war. You are an agricultural seed manufacturer facing some particularly aggressive price competition from new entrants to the market. One of your biggest customers is demanding price concessions, threatening to jump ship to one of these new, lower-priced competitors. How do you know if his threat is hollow and he's just blowing smoke or he's dead serious and your business is at risk? How can you tell if you'll actually be able to avoid a price war? For which customers do you need to provide a lower price and which ones will you retain without "laying bags of gold" at their feet (as Harry Stonecipher, former Boeing CEO, once said)?

Decision 4: Global pricing decisions. You are contemplating implementing zone pricing (pricing that varies by region or city) or perhaps modifying an existing global zone pricing strategy. How different should your prices be across the zones, and how should you customize prices on a country-by-country basis? How do you decide?

Decision 5: Sales force discretionary pricing—do you leave money on the table? You've traditionally given your sales force fairly wide latitude on setting prices out in the field. However, you're beginning to wonder how much you might be leaving on the table by allowing them to do this. Do they price too low in order to make the sale? Can you adjust their discretionary pricing bands in order to more closely align final sales terms with your customers' willingness to pay? And how do you know what individual customers *are* willing to pay? How can you adjust prices on an individual basis to maximize value extraction in the channel?

Decision 6: Your brand. You have believed for years that your brand should—and perhaps does—command a price premium in the market, but you aren't really sure how much it is actually worth. How much of a premium can you charge for your brand above all other objective attributes—and how does this valuation vary by individual customer? In fact, does it vary at all? How much more can you charge customer X versus customer Y—and why?

Decision 7: Reacting to competition. You want to be competitive and a leader in the market. Yet you seem to always be *reacting* to your competitors' moves. How do you stay one step ahead of the competition and dictate market terms so that they are reacting to you rather than the other way around? How do you incentivize your competitors to do what is in *your* best interest?

Decision 8: New product development and product launches. You have a very good research and development group; however, you would like them to focus their R&D efforts more closely on the market. After all, "Good companies have a single-minded obsession with following the money." How do you prioritize R&D efforts in line with customer-valued attributes, that is, how do you get them to concentrate on the areas where customers are willing to spend money?

Or, perhaps you have a new offering with features that you are not quite sure how to price. You don't want to introduce the product with the metaphorical party to which no one comes, but you don't want to leave money on the table. So, how do you decide on an appropriate price, and how might you price differently for individual customers? How can you distinguish pricing between the various service components?

Or maybe your task is to select appropriate production levels for your latest offering. How do you accurately and precisely predict the offering's post-launch market share? How might you accurately anticipate—and account for—your competitors' reactions to this new offering? And how might you encourage the reactions that are best for *your* business?

So, what do all of these decisions have in common? The common link is that they are all things that you can address—and answer/ measure, for that matter—via various applications of choice analysis. Choice analysis is based on detailed economic models of customer choice intended to get accurate information about an *individual* customer's willingness to pay for your product, brand, and so forth. We combine the information from Choice Analysis here with market-level knowledge to provide tactics that managers can use to minimize risk and maximize the likelihood of success.

While choice analysis is widely used in consumer markets, it is a vastly underutilized tool in B2B markets. Indeed, it is perhaps one of the most useful tools for differentiating your customer insights from those of your competition in these markets. Companies can use these tools to estimate numerous preferences for *each* customer and gain true customer insight that includes (but certainly is not limited to) the following:

- How much the company's brand is worth.
- How wide discretionary sales force pricing bands should be.
- How best to frame the price.
- How to price based on customer value.
- How to vary global pricing efforts.
- How to tailor marketing and pricing efforts to individual customers.

When combined with the principles of game theory (which are discussed throughout this book), choice analysis provides extraordinarily valuable (and underutilized) insight, thereby providing a substantial opportunity in B2B markets. Choice theory, choice analysis, and game theory interact in a manner that presents strategic opportunities. Delving into this is the essential theme that runs throughout this book—and a huge opportunity screaming to be employed in business markets today.

Choice Analysis and Customer Insight, Quantified

Imagine the following. You are selling a product or service to multiple buyers through traditional means (sales force, direct, a value-added reseller, whichever channel(s) you currently sell through). Your competitor has offered a better warranty (or whatever attribute best fits your current competitive situation). You decide to match it without knowing whether your customers truly value the extra savings, because you worry that you'll be at a disadvantage if you don't. In addition, your sales force is pressuring you to match the competitor's warranty since your customers are asking them to match the competition. And of course your customers would say that it was important to them for you to match your competitor's actions. After all, it doesn't cost *them* anything for you to extend the warranty terms. Does this sound familiar?

You believe that your customers care about certain attributes—including your brand, expertise, and service and/or sales team. However, you've always wondered how correct your impressions are and how strong their preferences are for one element over another. You also assume that your brand is important to your customers as well as the level of support you've offered—and that they value the relationship you've built over the years. But you aren't quite sure that you're assuming correctly or how much these factors impact their decision to stay with you versus moving to a competitor.

How much is all of this really worth? Your customers often complain about price, but you never know how serious they are or whether they're bluffing. How can you know with any precision?

Rizzutoism in practice: How most companies assess what customers want.

Many rely on a combination of ad hoc diagnostics: focus groups, sales team input, customer facing contacts, customer service, formal surveys, and customer insight tools. Some even get more sophisticated, developing metrics that show per customer margin or customer lifetime value. But none of these tools tells you whether you are charging the right price. Is it so high that if you lower it by a certain amount, you would gain enough customers to increase overall profit? Or is it so low that you are leaving money on the table? In the back (or perhaps forefront) of your mind, you wonder how accurate your customer intelligence is. Yet, you don't have the time, resources, or tools to ascertain this information with more precision. Perhaps it is just easier to copy our competitors' prices.

Well, this is nonsense. We can do better.

The very thought of asking customers what they want—whether via focus groups or in customer discovery, customer insight or willingness to pay surveys—is a Rizzutoism in practice, yet it's a big business today. Just think about the concept of sitting down with customers who have a vested interest in the session's outcome and using their feedback to plan your approach moving forward.[2] Would that have worked for Apple's Steve Jobs, Starbucks' Howard Schulz, or virtually any of the recent successful product introductions that have led innovation and growth? And what do you even get out of such exercises? What customers *think* they want, which has been conditioned by what *already exists* in the market. As a result, companies give customers what they think they want and end up "stuck in an undifferentiated mass of bland."[3] Clearly, the traditional methods for gathering customer input have some practical use at the early stages of development in terms of idea generation and qualitative reactions. But, as a rule, they are impractical as a basis for developing a strategy and certainly not useful for informing the detailed tactics that come out of that strategy.

Let's first understand precisely what is wrong with relying exclusively on these ad hoc diagnostics—focus groups, sales team input, customer facing contacts, customer service, formal surveys, and customer insight tools. They are all useful tools; the problem is that they are often the only type of customer diagnostic that many companies—particularly those in the B2B space—actually employ. To illustrate, imagine you are looking to buy a new automobile and you see two cars on the dealer's lot that are identical in every way except for the color; one is red and one is blue. The salesperson asks you how much more you are willing to pay for the red color, since you have a preference for red over blue. Would you answer honestly? Of course not; you don't want the salesperson to know you *really* want that red one. Now, what if a third party interviewed you on your way home from the lot (much like an exit poll in the political arena)? Would you be honest then? Maybe. And could you really, honestly, assess how much a red car was worth versus an identical blue one? Would this match what you would actually do at point of sale? It turns out that, for most people, the answer to these last two questions would be no. Even if we try, we don't do a particularly good job assessing our own willingness to pay for features, attributes, brands, and even for a product overall.

However, given the choice in practice—often referred to as "revealed preferences" since we reveal our preferences vis-à-vis our actions we can make choices—we can usually make a decision. So, offer us a red car at one price point and a blue car at a somewhat lower price point, and we actually can decide which one to purchase. Of course, our choice will depend upon the size of the difference between the two prices and how strong our preference is for a red as opposed to a blue car. This trade-off is precisely the type of choice that we make every day. And while we may not be able to quantify precisely how much red versus blue is worth to us, we can most certainly make a choice between two identical cars of different color at different price points. This is the essence of how and why choice analysis works. And, although it can be quite technical in nature, it is not this book's aim to provide technical detail (there are many other books that do), but rather this book aims to provide intuition and business applications and context, as the example below addresses.

Choice analysis, a form of stated preference analysis (since your preferences are "stated" in the study as opposed to being "revealed" in the market), uses these types of trade-offs in an experimental setting that allows us to statistically estimate—precisely and reliably—the value associated with each part of the offering (color, brand, and so forth).[4] It does so by presenting individuals with a series of product profiles or descriptions where each pair of profiles is designed in such a way as to isolate a trade-off between two attributes.[5] The choices made and systematic design of the options presented make it possible to statistically quantify the trade-offs that each respondent makes on each attribute. The result, on both an individual and market basis, is the ability to know how much customers value each attribute (and whether they do at all). The trade-off induced choices tell us how much each feature is worth to each individual.[6]

This approach (under the narrower heading of "conjoint analysis") has been used in consumer settings for well over 40 years now. It's a well-established tool for reliably estimating customer preferences and uses a combination of experimental design techniques borrowed from biology and medicine sciences, as well as choice models from economics and advanced statistical methods.

Examples of Notable Choice Analysis Projects

- A major airline manufacturer used choice analysis to assess the key features to include in new flight operations and maintenance training for 140 major airlines worldwide.
- A biotechnology agricultural seed company used the results of a detailed choice analysis of customers to decide

on which brands to consolidate and which to keep under a parent umbrella brand.

- The Alaskan tourist board studied the impact of deforestation on ecotourism in Alaska and was able to assess economic loss to the state as a result of deforestation.
- Boeing decided to stop development of the next generation Concorde (the Sonic Cruiser) after a choice analysis clearly suggested that customer willingness to pay for reduced trans-Atlantic flight time was not enough to support ongoing development costs.
- A major agricultural chemical manufacturer conducted choice analysis inside the channel to understand pricing in the wake of generic entry. It put in place a customized offering and pricing plan that helped fend off revenue loss from new generic entrants.
- American Public Radio (now American Public Media) conducted a detailed choice analysis across member stations in advance of raising prices after financial analysis suggested that donations and current revenue could not continue to support ongoing operations. Revenues were up almost 40 percent two years later as a direct result.

The following example helps convey precisely how choice analysis works. Note that there are numerous ways to conduct such studies and that this is just one (very) simple example. Imagine you are going on a vacation to a tropical island somewhere with your usual vacation companion(s). Your favorite travel website has given you some choices in regards to places to stay. There are two hotels—one a Hyatt, one under the brand name of John's (billed as a local favorite). They have identical room choices: each has an ocean or marsh view and either a twin or a king-size bed. The prices of the hotels range from $125 to $175 to $225 per night.

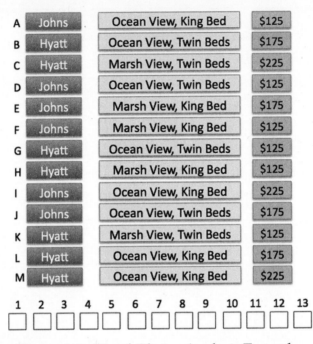

Figure 6.1   Hotel Choice Analysis Example.

Now imagine that you have to rank the list of 13 hotels (see Figure 6.1) from 1 (best) to 13 (worst) with instructions that read as follows:

You are planning an annual weeklong holiday to your favorite beach resort. You are in the process of deciding upon which hotel to stay at during your holiday. You are considering a variety of options and have come up with a list of 13 hotels that are available in the area you want to stay. Please rank the 13 hotels described on the next pages from 1 to 13 where 1 represents your best rating, that is, the option that you would most likely select and a 13 represents your lowest rating, the option that you would least likely select. Note that, except for the attributes listed below, the hotels are identical in every way.

Figure 6.1 represents one way of presenting this choice—albeit the simplest way by far. These trade-offs are more commonly presented using computers that adapt to earlier choices (adaptive conjoint models) or allow "none of the above" options. They're also conducted using card sort techniques, where the respondent sorts printed cards with full profile product descriptions that involve these trade-offs.[7]

We can use the results that come out of such analysis to make predictions with startling accuracy. To illustrate, note that we can examine the results for any one individual or for the market as a whole. Let's begin with the individual and take the case of Ashley, who filled out the above survey instrument in the following order (from most to least preferred): ADGFHKLBJEMIC. The instrument's specific (orthogonal) design allows us to use regression analysis to analyze Ashley's ordering, since the design forced her to make trade-offs along the way. And since we know which ones she eliminated, we can quantify the relative contribution of each attribute to her decision and test which matter versus which do not. As it turns out, the only things that mattered to Ashley were price and the type of view. The brand name and type of bed had no material impact on her choice decision.

Imagine being able to tell, *with accuracy*, which attributes matter to each customer—and then being able to deliver this information to the sales teams in the field. To be able to know how much your brand is worth (or not worth) on a customer-by-customer basis. To know when you're truly in danger of losing a customer who is clamoring for a price cut or whether there is something else you can do to keep that customer in the fold.

Figure 6.2 illustrates Ashley's results. Any feature that has a bar to the right of the 0 line affected Ashley's choice positively and anything to the left, negatively.[8]

We interpret each coefficient relative to the missing or base level for each attribute.

- "PRICE175" coefficient of –5.6 (see Figure 6.2) means that all else being equal, if a hotel was priced at $175 instead of $125

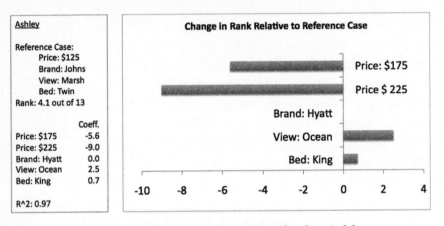

Figure 6.2   Choice Analysis Results for Ashley.

(the base case), then Ashley would have ranked it 5.6 points lower on this 13-point ranking scale. If it were priced at $225 instead of $125, she would have ranked it whopping 9.0 units lower out of the 13 possible rankings, a significant impact. Price clearly matters to Ashley.

- If the hotel had an ocean (marsh) view rather than a marsh (ocean) view, it would have been ranked 2.5 places higher (lower) in the 13-point rankings, all else being equal. Thus, type of view matters to Ashley, but not as much as price.

- As noted previously, the brand name and type of bed made no difference at all to Ashley in determining her 13-point rankings.

Imagine conducting a similar—and probably much more complicated—study in your industry of your customers. What attributes would you examine? Which customers would you want this type of information from? Would the information obtained help with the sales process, with price negotiations?

Indeed, a major advantage of this approach is that it is possible to examine every individual's choice decision for every conceivable combination of attributes—those that are technically feasible, for example. So, we can (quite reliably) predict what choice each individual in the sample would make when presented with these choices—and do so for any possible set of product offerings in the market, even those that are not currently offered. Imagine, for instance, being able to design an offering with the attributes that maximized market share, or being able to tell your sales teams what each customer cares about and how they make their decisions with precision and reliability or anticipate the impact of a competitor introduction.

Now, recall the eight decisions listed at the beginning of the chapter. You'll remember that one case featured a firm in the agricultural chemicals market that was facing new generic entry into the market. This was a real example. One large customer of a major supplier was threatening to jump ship to a lower priced generic alternative if a substantial price reduction didn't occur immediately. Yet this customer didn't know that we had just conducted a choice analysis with him a few weeks earlier (he hadn't made the connection), and the company knew from this analysis that he wasn't particularly price sensitive. It was really the technical knowledge and support that he valued. Hence, the company held its price firm, and he is still its number two revenue-generating customer today. Knowing when price-sensitive customers are ready to jump to the competition and when they are not can be an invaluable piece of information that prevents money from being left on the table.

Often, the toughest part of the process is getting to the decision maker. We did a study for Kodak a number of years ago, examining decision makers at over 2,100 research labs, hospitals, and factories. We asked a question on something we termed an individual's "degree of say" in the purchase decision. So, if you alone made the purchase decision, the degree of say would be 100 percent, you and someone else might be 50 percent each. It turns out that the average degree of say across the people interviewed at the 2,100-plus institutions totaled 275 percent—another Rizzutoism! If accurate and honest, degree of say should total 100 percent at every firm studied. How can you even tell *who's* making decisions in a situation like that?

Another challenge in implementation of choice analyses can often be the scarcity of time of decision makers. Can you imagine asking a top surgeon for 30 minutes of his or her time to answer a few questions—or even having to *pay* for their time? A colleague of mine came up with one innovative way of addressing this. He was implementing a study for a new hip replacement device that saved time in the operating theater. Since surgeons are notorious for guarding their time, this colleague set up shop at the annual conference for this type of surgery, where, as many of us know, they often serve bad coffee on breaks. He set up a very popular booth offering free espressos, lattes, and cappuccinos. Then, while waiting in line to get the free coffee, the surgeon was approached with the question: "While the milk froths, would you mind filling out a brief survey?" The amount of information they collected listening to the surgeons debate among themselves—in addition to the choice analysis results—was astoundingly valuable. Sometimes a little creativity is needed to get the results you're seeking!

HBO's *Barbarians at the Gate* was a business-based movie starring James Garner that I referenced earlier in the book to describe what a Rizzutoism would look like in practice. This movie—along with some of the experiences noted previously—has motivated us to develop a script for our own movie, which, like *Barbarians at the Gate*, is based on a real business setting. Now under review at a major Hollywood studio, the setting of one of the scenes and the rough script reads as follows:

Scene: *Conference room at one of the top 100 airlines in the world*[9]

Players:

1. Airline: *Head of Flight Operations*
2. Manufacturer: *Account Lead from Embraer, Boeing, or Airbus*

Script:

Manufacturer: *Thank you for taking the time to meet with us today. We are very interested in your views on how we can serve you better and design offerings that meet your needs more closely. We have designed an exercise, a card sort, to get the conversation going.*

Airline: Finally! I've waited for years for you to sit down at a table and actually listen to me and want to know what I think! Let's get started.

The manufacturer's lead representative explains the conjoint exercise and the head pilot in the organization begins to sort cards, examining the trade-offs across the orthogonally designed cards. He pauses and then calls in to his number two guy in the next office.

Airline: Joe [the number two pilot in the organization], what do you think of these two? Which one would we prefer? I really like the new display on this one, but the price is a bit steep. Would we go for it?

You get the idea. This meeting, based a true story, was scheduled for 30 minutes. After 90 minutes, it was still going strong, and the manufacturer account lead was unable to stop the rich and spirited conversation about the airline's needs. The head pilot called the manufacturer account lead three additional times later that week to discuss various nuances of the conversation. Talk about getting to know your customer!

While this may be a pretty boring script were we to really develop such a movie, it highlights one of the many benefits of integrating choice analysis into your customer insight program. All too often companies invest heavily in customer insight programs, only to do 90 percent of the work for 10 percent of the benefit. Integrating choice analysis—and all of the information and discussion that it generates—inside of existing customer insight and survey approaches can generate substantially greater benefits.

More generally, once you get to the decision makers, the information can be extraordinarily valuable—sometimes even more so than the choice results itself. This is why it is often advisable to have the sales teams in the field—the ones who own the relationship on the ground—actually implement the study. It can help build the relationship with the customer, engender buy-in from the sales teams, and ultimately generate a wealth of additional information.

We can also examine the results collectively to get a detailed sense of the overall market. We can plot each respondent in the previous example on two dimensions to get a graphical picture of the market as a whole—as Figure 6.3 demonstrates. Note that each dot represents a respondent—the person or company that provided the responses to the choice analysis. We can examine each dot more closely by cross-referencing its position on the chart relative to the corresponding individual result.

By studying Figure 6.3, we can identify segments or clusters of customers, find common threads that run through the segments and simulate various potential offerings, market outcomes, or competitive moves in order to accurately predict what would happen in the market before it actually does. Essentially these "market simulators" work to predict what choice each individual in the sample would make given

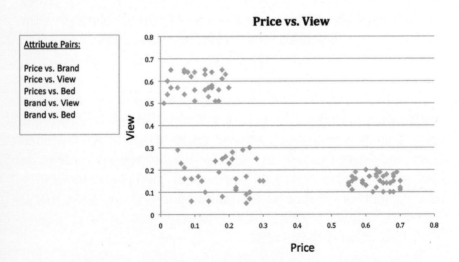

Figure 6.3   Choice Analysis Results for Ashley.

the scenario at hand (for example, reduce price, a competitive move, a new product launch, and so on). This allows companies to be able to—within some reasonable bounds—accurately predict what the market outcome will look like. These market simulators have been shown to be quite reliable predictors of actual market outcomes.[10]

Order matters. Use it to your advantage.

Research—Be Wary of Sales Force Intelligence

An interesting story regarding consumer intelligence has emerged from recent research (Coviello, Putsis, and Tipping, University of North Carolina at Chapel Hill working paper, 2012). The oilfield drilling services industry is an interesting one with, as you might imagine, given that it's the *oil* industry, a number of fascinating characters. Major competitors include French company Schlumberger, Halliburton (where Dick Cheney was chairman and CEO from 1995 to 2000) and Baker Hughes International. If you have seen the movie *The Aviator* starring Leonardo DiCaprio as Howard Hughes, you may recall a scene where Hughes talks about the possibility of failure in aviation, which meant that he'd have to go back to the oil business (apparently, a huge punishment—the Hughes portion of Baker Hughes was started by Howard Hughes's father)!

Fast forward to 2011: one of the smaller players in the industry had a new product to launch that it believed had significant benefit to customers, as it would substantially reduce drilling time for certain highly valued offshore drilling operations. Consequently, the company believed that demand price sensitivity would be low and willingness to pay high. The problem was that the company didn't know how much to charge for this new offering.

(continued)

(continued)

The company then conducted three waves of detailed choice analysis of customers' valuation of the attributes that the new drill would bring to the table. The first wave, very surprisingly, showed a great deal of price sensitivity and not a lot of willingness to pay. However, the second and third waves showed exactly what the company had expected—a high willingness to pay for the new offering and little price sensitivity. So, what do you think explained the difference between the expected results on waves two and three and the unexpected result in the first wave?

It turns out that the sales force in the field had answered the first wave's questions on behalf of their customers! They filled out the questionnaire thinking they knew what their customers would say, whereas the second and third waves were actually filled out by their customers.

Be wary of what you hear. Especially from your sales teams.

Finally, a major drawback is the lack of integration of game-theoretic considerations—a market simulator concept allows for examination of what-if scenarios. However, this is a far cry from integrating choice analysis (hopefully in more detail and more rigorously constructed than the simple example just described) into a well-constructed, strategic game theory exercise. We want to incentivize the competition to do what is in our best interest and stay one step ahead rather than one step behind.[11]

Chapter Summary and Key Business Principles

- Simply asking what your customers prefer in a focus group will not provide real customer insights. Actionable and accurate customer intelligence comes from choice analysis, where customers make trade-off purchase decisions.

- This technique is vastly underutilized in B2B markets. Therefore, companies that do undertake it have a huge potential competitive advantage.
- Choice analysis studies can also be used to strengthen the sales relationship with customers quite effectively.
- The process of choice analysis can be used to:
  - Design survey instrument focusing on all relevant attributes.
  - Perform detailed statistical analysis on each respondent.
  - Quantify preference for each attribute.
  - Segment the market; ascertain optimal design, pricing, etc.
- Choice analysis is based on a very rich and detailed theory developed over the past 50 years and has a powerful tradition in consumer markets. It can answer questions such as:
  - How much the company's brand is worth.
  - How wide discretionary sales force pricing bands should be.
  - How best to frame the price.
  - How to price based on customer value.
  - How to vary global pricing efforts.
- Do not simply accept surveys, focus groups, or willingness to pay (WTP) assessment in any tactical decision—we can do better and we should.

Key Business Tools

- Stated preference models
- Choice theory and choice analysis
- Optimal customer decision models
- Optimal pricing, product design simulations
- Competitive gap analysis
- Competitive and capabilities map

Vertical Incentive Alignment and Asset Specificity

It's All About Aligning Incentives
—P&G and the "Barney Relationship"[1]

One of the key focal areas in business today rests with what I will refer to as vertical incentive alignment. This is a term for designing relationships so that the incentives of all players are aligned with your best interest, in other words, so that your buyers and suppliers have your best interest at heart by virtue of the structural relationship that you have established. Perhaps the best example of this is Procter & Gamble's work in the early 1990s.

P&G shifted to what we know today as a key accounts system in the early 1990s. However, for most of its existence, P&G was organized along product lines, both internally and externally facing. Product managers—typically MBAs that are hired into an assistant brand manager position and, if successful, promoted to manage the brand—were micro-tasked. This essentially meant that brands were subdivided finely. Ivory soap had one brand manager, while Ivory dish soap had another. Pampers' boys small, medium, and large each had its own brand manager. Sales teams were also organized by product lines—examples included health and beauty, household products, and so on. Traditionally, sales teams would call on retailers by product lines—so, a health and beauty sales rep would call on the K-Mart buyer, a household product manager sales rep would call on the K-Mart buyer, and so on, across all the product lines that P&G carried.

This worked well when P&G held the balance of power in the manufacturer–retailer relationship. However, during the late 1980s and early 1990s, the U.S. retail environment went through significant consolidation, led in large part by Walmart (Walmart's compound annual growth rate (CAGR) from 1995 to 2001 was 9.3 percent, Albertson's CAGR over this period was 28.8 percent, both phenomenal growth rates). In fact, by the time we hit 1990, Walmart was running as much as one-third of P&G's nationwide sales of some categories through its doors.

P&G's response to this consolidation was one of the most brilliant business moves across all industries over the entire the decade of the 1990s. It proposed developing a key accounts system—a commonplace approach today—and set it up in a way that aligned incentives with its primary customer, Walmart. It began by renting office space nearby Walmart's world headquarters in Bentonville, Arkansas, and staffing it with a team of three of its very best people. It then asked Walmart to appoint three of *its* best people to help P&G's team design the relationship in any way that suited Walmart's best interests.

The team of six people had six months to structure the relationship pretty much any way Walmart wanted. They started with a one-page "Document of Trust" that detailed how all parties were interested in furthering both firms' joint interest in a mutually beneficial fashion and how they were building a long-term relationship that entailed trust between the two parties.

At first glance, this sounds like a simple, albeit pragmatic response by P&G; after all, Walmart's business had grown to as much as one-third of sales in some categories. However, P&G knew that simply positioning itself outside Walmart's headquarters and forming a close connection wouldn't be enough—this wasn't what relationships in business were *really* about. P&G understood that this was not a sustainable competitive advantage—and the reason why I derisively refer to such structures as a "Barney Relationship." Many of us remember the kids' show featuring the purple dinosaur, Barney. The theme song to that show went something like "I love you, you love me . . ." Well, "I love you" is great in kids' shows, but give Walmart a better deal and it'll walk on "I love you" every time.

The key in business relationships that many firms miss is that the key isn't the relationship itself. Relationships can be fleeting; people come and go, inferior products give way to superior offerings, and so forth. The key, therefore, resides in turning the relationship into something *sustainable*—often employing something called "asset specificity."

Herein lies the beauty of P&G's strategy. It said to Walmart, "We're not interested in *just* being your friend; we want to help you run your business more *efficiently*." As soon as Walmart hears the "E" word, it begins listening. What P&G proposed was for both firms to invest in an inventory control management system—one that they would own, manage, and run jointly. They would invest together in a system that would track inventory on each and every P&G product sold in the United States. They would establish specified stock levels; this way, if one of P&G's products went below a pre-specified stock level in one of Walmart's stores, P&G would show up just in time at that Walmart store and replenish the stock of inventory on hand. Walmart would never (or at least almost never) run out of P&G stock. Further, P&G estimated that Walmart's inventory holding costs on P&G products would be reduced by about 60 percent, a figure that turned out to be roughly correct.

So, why was this one of the most brilliant business moves in the decade of the 1990s? In order to appreciate this, we need to understand what this system did to both parties' incentive structure—the key to understanding the dynamics of any channel relationship.

First, what did Walmart gain from such a system? What was in it for the retailer? Clearly, having one of your major suppliers take on inventory supply and reduce your inventory holding cost by as much as 60 percent has to be an attractive feature since holding inventory is one of the most expensive parts of doing business for a retailer. It's also highly desirable for your supplier to contribute financially to a system that you were planning on investing in anyway. Further, this has the potential to enable you to push (read: squeeze) similar requests (read: demands) down onto other manufacturers. Clearly, there is little downside from Walmart's perspective.

Now, what was in it for P&G—and why was it so brilliant? Clearly, one benefit was the company's ability to solidify an essential relationship with its most important customer. And we know that despite their importance, these relationships don't always last. Another benefit to P&G was the timely information to which it now had access. It could see sales in real time, getting almost-instant feedback on what sold well where. In fact, P&G estimated that it was able to offset the higher distribution and logistics costs thanks to the increased production and distribution efficiencies that it gained from this information. P&G could also adjust its product mix for regions of the country, even down to the individual store level.[2] This made planning future product mix and emphasis more efficient.

However, we still haven't gotten to the real benefit: the reason why it was such a brilliant business move.

The most important advantage for P&G is what the system did to alter Walmart's incentive structure, which is always the key in understanding and designing optimal channel structure. A retailer is motivated by a number of things, but margins and turns are clearly two important items. So consider what this system did to Walmart's incentive structure in terms of these two elements. Margins are essentially retail price minus wholesale price minus transaction cost, which includes the cost of holding inventory. By reducing the inventory holding costs on P&G products alone by approximately 60 percent, Walmart's margins on P&G products went through the roof. Further, by streamlining inventory, the turn rate on P&G products just increased substantially, as well. What does Walmart want to do as a result? Sell more P&G product, sell more P&G product, sell more P&G product—and put Unilever products on the back shelf where no one can see them. (I am exaggerating, of course, but not by much.)

P&G has perfectly aligned its own incentives with its behemoth of a number one customer—all with a (relatively) small investment in the inventory control system. Better yet, P&G does not have to do anything other than sit and watch after the system is in place. It does not have to monitor what happens, attempt to assess Walmart's adherence to any contractual agreement, and so on. Why? Because P&G knows that Walmart will do what is in P&G's best interest since it is in Walmart's best interest to do what is in P&G's best interest. Brilliant.

Now, some questions naturally arise:

1. Why didn't other manufacturers do the same? Wouldn't Walmart want that? Clearly, this would happen in time. However, the original architecture at the time was a closed proprietary system (this was 1990, after all). It would take time—almost five years to be exact—for competitors to establish systems similar to that of P&G. P&G was staying one step ahead by sequentially rolling out similar systems to other retailers, one-by-one. It took until the end of the decade before all competitors had broken in across the board.[3]

2. Wouldn't Walmart eventually win and squeeze all manufacturers? Didn't Walmart win in the long run? Yes and yes. However, this was inevitable in 1990; it was just a matter of time. Give me, in a low-margin, intensely competitive market, a 5 to 10 year competitive advantage knowing that I will get squeezed anyway in the long run—and I'll take it every time.

3. Why did Walmart allow P&G to gain in this fashion? Because it won as well. P&G's brilliance was in recognizing that Walmart benefited from this structure as well.

P&G used the concept of *asset specificity*[4] to its advantage, something that firms are using more and more in the channel to their strategic advantage in what we will term "virtual vertical integration." Asset specificity is technically defined as assets that are unique or specific to a firm, relationship, or joint venture. In this context, however, we define it as follows:

A joint investment, often well short of a full-blown merger or acquisition, unique to the parties at hand, that aligns the incentives of both parties.

So, what are the lessons to be learned from all of this? And how can you determine where this might be a possibility for your business? Start by considering the following:

- What inevitable trends in your industry would, if you take advantage now, give you a competitive advantage, even if only in the short run? How might you turn this into a sustainable long-term competitive advantage as P&G did by sequentially staying ahead of the competition?

- Use the notion of asset specificity to your advantage. The first step is to identify the part of the value chain in which you are competing, as well as gaps in competencies required to compete effectively there or to access a key strategic control point. Subsequently, use the concept of asset specificity where possible to align the incentives across the board. Don't immediately think in terms of merger and/or acquisition. You may be able to achieve the same end with a substantially smaller investment (and managerial headache).

- Remember that managing customers and suppliers (what we will call vertical relationships) is all about incentive structure. First and foremost, spend time understanding where the power is in the channel and what incentivizes each player in the value chain.

- Use this to your strategic advantage by tying these incentives to your ultimate objective of maximizing profits in the market's high-priority segments.

Note that such an investment doesn't have to involve technology and inventory management systems—a concept best illustrated by the distribution system that Anheuser-Busch established. Located in St. Louis, Missouri, the brewing company has established a network of what is often referred to as "dual exclusive territorial monopolies." This means that Anheuser-Busch grants local distributors the exclusive right to distribute its brands (including Budweiser, Michelob, Busch, and others) in a given geographic region.

For example, Tom Ryan Distributing in Flint, Michigan,[5] has exclusive territorial rights to sell Anheuser-Busch beer in Michigan's Genesee and Lapeer counties. The company also offered attractive financing and dealer support to Tom Ryan's operations, including joint investment in part of the physical infrastructure. In return, Anheuser Busch asked that Tom Ryan represents their brand well and that Tom Ryan sells only Anheuser-Busch products.[6] This is a pretty good setup for Tom Ryan, considering that Anheuser-Busch products command close to a 50-percent market share in Genesee County.

Flint, Michigan, is a very blue-collar town, dominated by General Motors, members of the United Auto Workers union, and related businesses and industries. When *Money* magazine had its very first issue dedicated to the best places to live in the United States, it listed the 301 most populous cities in the country from 1 (most preferred) to 301 (least preferred). Flint ranked dead last at 301. The president of the Miller distributor in the area once said to me that selling beer in Flint was great—"if times are good we sell a lot of beer; if times are bad, we sell even more beer."

This should give a sense of what selling beer in the Flint, Michigan, area has been like over the years—and why such a structure might be so valuable. It aligns the two parties' incentives, much like the inventory control system of P&G. Tom Ryan Distributing has one goal: sell Anheuser-Busch beer. Local distributors take great care to protect the Anheuser-Busch brand—and for very good reason. Their interests are aligned with the interest of the brand umbrella and with the parent company. Note that Anheuser-Busch could have achieved essentially the same thing by owning its own distributors, but this is not one of its core competencies. Tom Ryan Distributing does a fantastic job catering to the local market, knowing each and every customer's needs, because it is a local institution. Anheuser-Busch cannot do this nearly as effectively from its headquarters in St. Louis—and it knows this. It also knows that any attempt to do so would not sit well in the heartland—particularly in cities like Flint. Anheuser-Busch achieves a better local on-the-ground presence and distribution working with a local distributor whose incentives are exactly aligned with its own via an investment that falls far short of what it would take to buy, own, and run its own distribution arm.

Both the P&G and the Anheuser-Busch examples highlight the use of a (relatively) small investment (short of a full-blown merger or acquisition) that aligns the incentives of both parties (think of the Anheuser-Busch example as the low-tech version of what P&G did). What investment—or asset specific to the relationship—would align conflicts in the value chain in *your* industry?

The following exercise will help you figure that out.

Exercise: Map out the value chain in your industry or sector. For each portion, list the key capabilities needed to compete effectively in that market. Next, list the competencies whereby your firm has an advantage (in green) or disadvantage (in red). Then, mark or circle the sections of the value chain that have the potential to be strategic control points. Once you've identified these—either high-margin areas where you have competitive advantage or where there may be potential for strategic control—list the principal ways in which you might control these areas of the value chain—for example, merger, acquisition, partner, joint venture. Is there a way to use the concept of asset specificity to gain a competitive advantage and align the incentives of key parties in these areas? Be imaginative. What did you learn?

Virtual Vertical Integration

Virtual vertical integration:

> *Integration across two (or more) firms whereby the form of the integration aligns the incentives of the firms involved. It can be in terms of materials (for example, inbound and outbound logistics), financial instruments (for example, automated payment systems),*

time, people and any operational aspect of the organization that can be made specific to the interests of both (or of multiple) parties, but does not generally involve asset transfer or acquisition.

Not surprisingly, virtual vertical integration almost always involves some sort of asset specific to the relationship between the parties involved; however, it doesn't necessarily have to. For example, financial integration (automated processing and invoice payment) may involve little or no joint ownership of an asset unique to the venture. However, if it can be *made unique* to the relationship of the two parties, it can align their incentives with few or no specific assets involved.

In order to see how all of this impacts business today in a bit more intuitive fashion, there are numerous examples of virtual vertical integration in practice we can look at. The classic example is that of P&G and Walmart discussed in detail earlier in this chapter. In this example, the joint investment in the inventory management system aligned the incentives of both parties without a formal merger. Nowadays, more recent examples are numerous: integrated materials management, automated payment systems, Square, the Starbucks iPhone app, the list goes on. Integrated materials management (IMM, integrating materials and processes throughout the value chain) imbeds the supplier's supply chain into the buyer's so that the seller knows supply lead times and inventory levels in real time. This reduces the effective cost on the buying side and often also reduces the cost on the supply side, making IMM something that benefits both parties and, accordingly, aligns the interests of both. The Starbucks app (and many other mobile payment systems such as Square) allows you to pay for your soy latte or venti black coffee with your phone. This makes it easier (and seemingly cheaper since you don't need money, just your phone) for the customer to choose Starbucks over some other rival brand, again aligning the interests of both Starbucks and its customers.

To illustrate how virtual vertical integration can motivate multiple organizations much the way full-blown vertical integration (vis-à-vis a merger or acquisition) can, we look to the aerospace industry. Its long history of things like integrated materials management and performance-based logistics (essentially paying for performance, not by the part or billing) are two examples of this. However, the capabilities for virtual vertical integration are currently just skimming the surface. With the advanced information and sensor capabilities onboard current aircraft, the plane itself knows if a part fails en route to a destination and can notify ground maintenance so that they can be on-site and ready to replace the part before the first passenger gets off the plane. The airline benefits because it's better able to utilize aircraft, which is obviously a crucial component of profitability. The maintenance firm benefits because it's able to know *to the minute* when the airline will need its staff—and parts allocation, inventory management, and so forth—at the gate. Using information in this way is a form of virtual vertical integration. Another way of obtaining the same degree of incentive alignment is for the airline to own its own maintenance and repair organization (MRO). Here, vertical incentive alignment vis-à-vis the materials management system achieves virtually the same thing without everything required in a physical merger. This is the key concept of virtual vertical integration, evident in all these examples.

There is one common theme inherent in much of virtual vertical integration: the use of information. The ability to combine information is what makes the jointly owned information the asset specific to the relationship. It is hard to believe, therefore, that firms that own data (such as a drilling company that compiles performance data in a well) will readily hand that information over to the client (such as a major oil company)—often for free. That information is a valuable asset that, if used properly, can form the basis of aligning the incentives of the parties to the information (for example, a drilling company such as Baker Hughes and an oil company such as Shell or Exxon Mobil).

Issues That Arise

Imagine the following—which we'll call "Scenario 1." You park your new BMW in the company parking lot in the morning and head into the office for a day at work. At the end of a long day of meetings, you get to your car to head home. You notice a note hanging from your car's rear view mirror from the BMW dealer that reads:

> *We noticed that your BMW 330i was due for its regularly scheduled service. When we cross-referenced our service department openings with your Outlook calendar, we noticed that your car wouldn't be used today. Accordingly, we took your car in for its scheduled service and include an itemized list of services performed here. A total of $547.49 has been billed to your MasterCard on file.*

We can address the question of whether this is an invasion of privacy by allowing you to opt in or out of such a service. However, perhaps the more relevant question is: Are there conflicting incentives that create "principal agent" problems between the dealer, service department, and customer? While it may be convenient to have your vehicle servicing done without the hassle of going to the dealer, dropping your car off and/or waiting around while the work is performed, how do you know your car *really* needed the service? How do you know that the dealer didn't perform more than was *actually required*? Certainly, the dealer has a financial incentive to do maintenance quicker than you might prefer under such an arrangement.

Contrast this to "Scenario 2," which provides the opposite incentive structure. In this case, BMW's system does not require maintenance at scheduled mileage intervals; rather, the maintenance schedule is based on your individual driving tendencies. So, if you drive your car hard, you might need a scheduled service earlier than the normal 20,000 miles; if you drive easy, you might be able to delay service beyond 20,000 miles. Further, BMW includes free regularly scheduled maintenance for the first 50,000 miles with every new car purchased. You know you need your standard 20,000-mile service because the light comes on your dashboard indicating "service required." This can come on at 17,000 miles or 24,500 miles or 20,000 miles, depending upon your driving habits.

Since BMW covers the cost of maintenance, how do you know that the dealer performs it when your car truly *needs* it and that it didn't delay it in a way that might not have any adverse short-term impacts but that could shorten the engine life, for example? BMW certainly has a different incentive than you do under this arrangement: its goal is to postpone service as long as possible, whereas yours is to have the service done as early as possible. There is an inherent conflict between the BMW dealer's interest (to earn a profit) and your interest (to save money and prolong the car's life).

The nature of the arrangement under Scenario 2 produces an inherent incentive conflict that is the opposite of that in Scenario 1. Under Scenario 1, the dealer's incentive to perform maintenance was *greater* than the car owner's; in Scenario 2, the dealer's incentive to perform maintenance was *less* than that of the car owner. The key in most markets, particularly within the channel, is to recognize that these types of incentives exist—and to work it to your competitive advantage.

Chapter Summary and Key Business Principles

- Always align incentives. The best type of business-to-business relationship is one that is mutually beneficial to the seller and the customer.

- Asset specificity refers to a specific investment that aligns the interests of the parties involved. Use the notion of asset specificity to your advantage—in a way that aligns incentives upstream and downstream.

- Identify key relevant areas in the value chain. Use the concept of asset specificity where possible to align the incentives across the board.

- Managing customers and suppliers (what we call vertical relationships) is all about incentive structure. First and foremost, spend time understanding where the power resides in the channel and what incentivizes each player in the value chain.
- What inevitable trends in your industry would give you a competitive leg up if you if you take advantage of them now—even if only in the short run? How might you turn these trends into a sustainable competitive advantage as P&G did by sequentially staying ahead of the competition?
- Use the notion of asset specificity as follows:
  - First, identify the part of the value chain in which you are competing on and pinpoint gaps in competencies required to compete effectively in that part or to access a key strategic control point. Once you've done so, use the concept of asset specificity where possible to align the incentives across the board.
  - Don't immediately think merger and/or acquisition. You may be able to achieve the same end with a substantially smaller investment (and managerial headache).
  - Managing customers and suppliers (what we call vertical relationships) is all about incentive structure. First and foremost, spend time understanding where the power is in the channel and what incentivizes each player in the value chain.
  - Use this to your strategic advantage by tying these incentives to your ultimate objective of maximizing profits to the high-priority segments in the market.

Key Business Tools

- Vertical incentive alignment
- Asset specificity
- Virtual vertical integration
- Analysis of structural power within the channel

CHAPTER
8

Setting Tactics in Today's Environment

The examples you've read throughout the book so far illustrate that it no longer makes sense to talk about the "4Ps" (product, price, place, and promotion) of marketing, now a very dated and antiquated concept. Today's environment is very different from the "push" approach of years past. Hence, this chapter focuses on the elements of today's markets that differ substantially from traditional legacy theories. A model that is much more relevant now is something we will call Five Points of Effective Tactics:

1. Points of *positioning*: unique and winning value propositions
2. Points in *time*: offering timing
3. Points of *value*: principles in extracting value
4. Points of *access*: points of customer access
5. Points of *touch*: customer touch as the embodiment of your strategy

Further, business models need to be reinforcing—the saying that you are only as good as your weakest link (or which wheel on the car is more important?) is so true in business. Let's briefly explore each of these in turn through the use of a true story.

The Story of the Whaling Ship Essex . . . Why What You Know May Be More Dangerous than What You Don't

The remarkable story of the journey of the 238-ton Nantucket-based whaling ship the *Essex* (that of *Moby Dick* fame) provides many lessons for business—especially in terms of the use (or misuse) of information.

The story began with much fanfare as the *Essex* left Nantucket in the year 1819. Imagine the crew about to leave port on this business trip: "Honey, I'm off. Be back in a couple of years . . ." Sadly, most of this crew never returned. On the morning of November 20, 1820, when the *Essex* was about 1,000 miles from the Galapagos Islands near the equator off the coast of Chile, a huge sperm whale attacked the ship twice,[1] sinking it with two powerful blows. Some accounts suggest that hammering to repair a broken mast had mirrored a whale's mating call, which is often met by attacks on rival mates.

As the ship sank, the crew gathered onto three smaller whaleboats with the goal of "sailing to the nearest island," according to the *Essex*'s Captain Pollard's written accounts. However, deciding precisely *where* the nearest island was proved to be a subject of debate amongst the crew—and continues to be debated even to this day. Knowing that whaleboats could only travel with the wind, the captain and crew conferred, with Captain Pollard concluding that the available options were as follows:

- Backtracking to the Galapagos Islands and, beyond that, to South America. This would entail bucking the southeasterly trade winds and a strong westerly current for over 2,000 miles—a journey the captain deemed impossible.

- Taking advantage of the winds by sailing to the West. The closest islands, the Marquesas, were about 1,200 miles away and would have been the easiest location to sail to. However, the Marquesas were rumored to be dark, dangerous islands filled with "fighting, cannibals, and homosexuals" according to accounts of the time and journal entries. Therefore, this was a location to be avoided at all costs.

- Further to the west were the Society Islands, about 2,000 miles away. Although the crew had no information about this location, Captain Pollard was under the impression that these islands were much safer, in part due to the comparison to the known dangers of the Marquesas. It was determined that this option would take about 30 days.

The first mate offered a dissenting view:

- They had absolutely no information about the Society Islands; they could be *worse*, for all they knew.
- There was a better alternative: travel south for about 1,500 miles to latitude 26° S. They believed that this part of the journey would take 26 days. From here, they would enter a band of variable breezes that they could ride to Chile or Peru so that they could be on the coast of South America and safety within an additional 30 days. They estimated that this journey, would take 56 days in total—and they had enough food to last 60. Though it wasn't a great margin for error, this was a known entity and, in theory, they had enough food to last.

The result—choosing the first mate's second option—turned out to be a fatal error in judgment, and one that cost the lives of most of the crew (although Captain Pollard did survive). What would *you* have done?

Of course, we can answer this with the benefit of 20/20 hindsight. But ironically, several months before the *Essex* departed from Nantucket, New Bedford mercenaries had come back to Massachusetts with an account of the Marquesas that they never relayed to Captain Pollard and the crew of the *Essex*. As it turns out, the Society Islands and Tahiti would have provided safety, rest, food, and tranquility, and had they chosen this route the result would almost certainly have been survival for most, if not all, of the crew.

Though it may not seem related at first glance, the lessons for business are clear and salient:

- A fear of the unknown can lead us to embrace the presumed safety of what is known, often with disastrous consequences.

Kodak knew film, not digital; Dell knew mass customization, not design and music; this list goes on.

- Research and access to information is crucial. Garnering meaning out of reams of data is more the norm nowadays than what used to be the norm—that is, a *lack* of data. Think of how sites like Facebook, Google, Amazon, LinkedIn, and others have to infer meaning out of the volumes of data they get by the second. Customer and competitive intelligence is at the forefront of B2C businesses today and provides a potential strategic advantage for B2B companies that utilize data—and the information it contains—effectively.

- Lack of information is not, in and of itself, a reason to disregard a strategic option. Of course, Captain Pollard and his crew couldn't wait until more information became available. But in business today, taking the time to make an informed decision can often be the metaphorical difference between making the fatal decision to travel to the coast of South America rather than to the friendly Society Islands and Tahiti.

- The opportunity cost of choosing only known strategic alternatives can be high. Do not limit the set of options you consider to what you already know. Get more information, hire more resources, do whatever it takes. Information is essential in the current economic environment.

- Sometimes fear of the cannibals should be your *last* concern, while fear of a lack of meaningful information should be your first.

Now, let's use this to think back to our Five Points of Effective Tactics:

1. Points of Positioning
2. Points in Time—Offering Timing
3. Points of Value—Value Extraction Considerations

4. Points of Access—Strategic Barriers to Entry and the Story of Blockbuster

5. Points of Touch—The Embodiment of Your Strategy

Points of Positioning

The example of Captain Pollard and the *Essex* illustrates many things, but the importance of information and the need for everything to go just right to succeed are two of the more important ones. Information is no less important in a business setting. The use of attribute positioning by way of choice theory, as noted earlier, is one such place where information is crucial to success.

One example that illustrates this point is that of an automobile manufacturer in the late 1980s that used attribute space analysis to determine that there was a potential opportunity in the United States for a small, inexpensive, reliable, fun-to-drive two-seater sports car. So, it went to the design team, R&D, and manufacturing and developed a design that was close to what was eventually introduced in the market.

There was one problem, however: the estimated production cost of this initial design was approximately $30,000—not exactly an *inexpensive* sports car even if it did meet all of the other criteria. As a result, the CEO at the time issued a mandate: he dictated that priority No. 1 for the company was to get production costs down. The marketing, R&D, design and manufacturing groups, previously siloed, began working closely together to find a way of integrating design, production, and assembly to drive down the cost to approximately $13,000 (which eventually came down substantially with volume production). The company won a number of awards for its computer-aided design and computer-aided manufacturing production interface; inventory management; and streamlined, innovative production processes. The result was the 1990 launch of what

Road & Track magazine called the "Car of the Decade for the 1990s": the Mazda Miata (MX5 in Europe).

The key to the success was originally spotting a market opportunity in attribute space. For had the company not been able to do this, all the production and process technology in the world wouldn't have resulted in its eventual success. Of course, the product would have failed without the production innovation, as well. Hence, good marketing entails bringing all of the pieces together, most often starting with observing a market need rather than using a core competency to push an idea onto the market. The success of the Miata speaks volumes about the importance of attribute space and the importance of having the box to think outside of in the first place. Even with the right information, success invariably requires iteration. Information and persistence are key ingredients.

Positioning today differs in that the use of a strategic control point is often a key ingredient in firms' positioning decisions. That is, positioning—as well as both strategy and tactics—is often interconnected. Walmart's supply chain hold enables its low-cost positioning; Southwest's all-737 fleet facilitates the low-cost carrier model; Amazon's grip across the supply chain enables it to extract higher margins in both its publishing and Marketplace businesses; and online real estate brokerage Redfin's access to the Multiple Listing Service is at the heart of its differentiation from tradition (we will discuss this in detail in Chapter 9). The list is nearly endless.

Points in Time—Offering Timing

Timing was everything for Captain Pollard; the decision as to where to head hinged in part on the number or days of food available relative to journey time. This is also the case for many of the examples outlined in this book. Many will wonder about the importance of being the first in regards to many of these cases. There is a great deal of research on what is often referred to as "first-mover advantage" (and sometimes disadvantage). While the companies that act quickly have the benefit of being first to market, they do so with a huge price: a large bull's-eye on their backs. Often, those that wait and learn from the first entrant's missteps can win out in the long run.

However, there is an important distinction to be made here. First movers in product areas, where attributes and features are (relatively) easy to imitate, can be at a disadvantage. This is because rivals can enter after the pioneer with improved and/or lower cost alternatives. On the other hand, those that move first and secure critical strategic control points—as illustrated by the Softsoap® pumps example in Chapter 4—do so to long-term strategic gain. Thus, *sustainable* first-mover advantage generally relates to strategic control points, not imitable attributes. And those that move early in an area should heed this lesson: if they can gain control of strategic control points, they'll have sustainable competitive advantages in the long run.

Lessons for Today's Market

- First-mover advantage in strategic control points is often significant and sustainable. Once a brand owns a control point, it is difficult to supplant.
- First-mover advantage on attributes alone is often easily imitated; unless you can find a point of strategic control, be careful.
- Be on time. Apple succeeded in the smartphone market in part because the relatively slow Edge technology had given way to 3G; Boo.com, which you'll read about next, didn't succeed in large part because it was *ahead* of its time. Timing, as they say, is everything.

Boo.com, founded by Ernst Malmsten, Kajsa Leander, and Patrik Hedelin in late 1999, is a classic example of poor entry timing and lack of strategic control. The site sold branded fashion apparel at discounted prices over the Internet (much like successful Internet retailers of today such as Net-a-Porter, Bluefly, and Ideeli.com). By various accounts, the company spent $180 million of venture capital in just 18 months and was placed into receivership on May 18, 2000, eventually liquidating. In June 2008, CNET hailed Boo.com as one of the greatest dot-com busts in history. Ernst Malmsten wrote about the experience in a book called *Boo Hoo: A Dot.com Story from Concept to Catastrophe*, published in 2001.[2] The tragedy of Boo.com's story isn't in its lavish spending on corporate jets or parties but on the *timing* of its venture. The failure had less to do with the dot-com bust in the early 2000s than it did with the narrow bandwidth, limited Internet penetration, and fledgling delivery network available at the time. The business models of Ideeli.com, Net-a-Porter.com and Bluefly.com are not fundamentally different from that of Boo.com; however, their infrastructures and Internet bandwidth are drastically so.

Timing, as they say, is everything. If you're Apple, you can fail with a Newton and learn from it. But if you only have one shot at the venture capital market and you are not Steve Jobs, you cannot. It is not just the offering alone that makes or breaks a company. In today's ever-connected world, it is the entire support business environment. In many ways, this book has emphasized taking the right kind of risks while avoiding the unnecessary ones—how to innovate while knowing where to focus and back rivals into a corner.

Points of Value—Value Extraction Considerations

In the early 2000s, Heinz's U.K. division hired a major consulting firm to assess customer-level response in the canned soup category (which was just the first of many categories they were planning to assess). The company amassed a wealth of data on purchasing behavior in the category over time and across retailers using scanner data from major U.K. retailers. After a detailed and comprehensive statistical demand analysis of purchase scanner data, it concluded that the demand elasticity in this category was –3.8. This means that, for example, a 10 percent drop in prices would drive an approximately 38 percent increase in volume.[3] In a category that is relatively flat in terms of cost curves and overall growth (it's difficult to get people to consume more soup through a drop in price alone) and that had a bit of over-capacity at the time, such a price cut seemed to make perfect sense to the managers at Heinz.

However, such an analysis and conclusion were not only incomplete and naïve, but downright silly. Why?

The answer is simple: were Heinz to cut prices by 10 percent—and therefore produce a nearly 40 percent increase in volume—close competitors Campbell and Baxter's would surely respond in kind. The net result of the original 10 percent price cut by Heinz would therefore have been all three competitors back at their original share positions—albeit at a 10 percent lower price point. The only winner out of the recommended strategy would have been the consumer; all three firms would have lost revenue and profits as a result of the recommended move!

Heinz learned the crucial lesson that companies need to create strategies that anticipate and shape competitor moves and responses, not ignore them.[4] Our strategic and tactical decisions do not exist in a vacuum, and we cannot presume that they do. We must choose our optimal strategies based on net and not initial market response. And it turns out that game theory provides us with the necessary tools to do exactly this.

One of the best examples of the strategic (game theoretic) use of information to extract value is as follows.[5] Imagine 20 people in a room, each of whom is holding a single red card. Imagine further that I am in front of the room holding 20 black cards. The 21 people in the room (20 plus me) are told that anyone holding one red and one black card (they don't have to be a pair as long as one is red and one is black) will receive $100. They are also told that everyone knows the number of cards, the number of players and the money involved.

I know that in order to earn any money, I need to obtain some red cards. So, I try to negotiate, in private, with one of the red cardholders—let's call her Jane—to buy a red card. The conversation might go something like this:

Me: *I'll give you $5.00 for your card.*

Jane: *No way.*

Me: *Okay, I'll give you $10.00.*

Jane: *Take a hike.*

Me: *Okay, my best and final offer—$20.00.*

Jane: *What part of no don't you understand?*

Where do you think this negotiation would end up on average across the 20 red cardholders and myself? Most people would agree that, on average, we'd end up at a 50/50 split of the $100.

Question: How do I find a way to make more money?

Well, one way of taking home more than half would be for me to tear up one of the black cards. Then, my threat is actually credible when I tell Jane I'm walking away from her after my best and final offer. This is because I have created scarcity. There is one fewer red card than there are black cards. Everyone in those private negotiations would fear that I would walk away and freeze them out completely, kind of like the old kids' game of musical chairs.

Question: What can the 19 do in response?

The most common answer that I get for this is for them to collude, that is, to agree to act in concert in negotiating with me. However, this is a *business* story with a *business* analogy, and collusion is, presumably, not an option.[6] So, what then should they do? Herein lies the moral of this example; what can they do is the wrong question! By the time I've torn up the one black card, it's too late; I have already destroyed value.

So, why was this the wrong question in the first place?

The correct solution in this example is to think ahead and not get into the situation where they would even need to worry about scarcity. That is, they should begin by providing me an incentive to never tear up that black card.

Let me explain. If the 20 other people had thought ahead and simply announced at the outset that they would immediately make public the results of any negotiation done in private, I never would have had the incentive to tear up the card in the first place. Even if I had broken off negotiations with Jane, the other 19 would have known it right away—and I would have been back to 19 on 19. Therefore, I wouldn't have been able to create scarcity by tearing up one black card!

Hence, had this announcement been made, I never would have had the incentive to tear up the card in the first place! The key here isn't just the power of information (although this is important). This story also emphasizes the need to think ahead and about incentives, rather than just react. Doing so would have enabled each of the 20 red cardholders to be in a better strategic position and presumably negotiate a better deal for themselves.

Winner's Curse

A related and important topic is that of the "winner's curse".[7] To illustrate this principle, imagine I have told you and a group of others that I have a Federal Reserve note in my pocket, but I haven't told you its denomination. I have let you know that it is not a $1 bill, nor is it a $100 bill or higher. So, I have a $5, $10, $20 or a $50 note in my pocket. You and 99 other people get to bid on the right to buy the Federal Reserve note in my pocket. What would you bid? Why? And who will win the right to buy what's in my pocket?

In order to answer this, we need to understand the distribution of expectations regarding what the 100 people (including you, of course) believe I have. Imagine, as illustrated in Figure 8.1, that 10 people think I have a $5 bill in my pocket; another 10 people are convinced that it's a $50 ("He *is* writing a book, after all!"); 25 people believe I have $10; and the remaining 55 people correctly believe that I have a $20 bill in my pocket (think about how would you have fared with this distribution). Who would have won the right to buy the Federal Reserve note in my pocket? It would have been 1 of the 10 who were convinced that I had a $50 note—and that individual would have lost money on winning the bid. It turns out that the winner's curse is inherent in any process like this. Think about it logically: even if the participants were correct *on average* and there is any distribution across that expectation, the winner will lose.

However, this is not unique to auctions; it plays out in everyday life, as well. An example from Barclays Bank in the United Kingdom from a few years back says a lot about human nature and the role of competitiveness. In the late 1990s and early 2000s, commercial

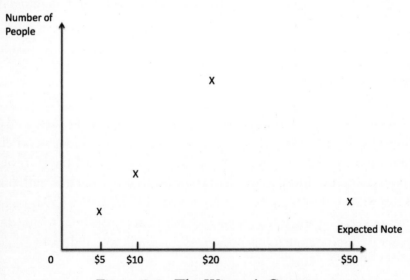

Figure 8.1   The Winner's Curse.

lending or the wholesale clients side of major banks in the United Kingdom competed vigorously for standing in the "league tables." When Barclays account managers knew that they were competing against NatWest—their main rival at the time—for a key account, it was as though they put blinders on: "Beat NatWest, beat NatWest, beat NatWest . . ." It was all they could think about. They wanted to win the competition at all costs, and this is something that plays out in competitive sales situations all of the time.[8] What would the best outcome of such a sales competition be? Clearly, that we win the competition with huge margins. The next best alternative is that we win the competition with acceptable margins. The next best outcome is that our competitor wins the competition, and loses money. And of course, the worst outcome is that we win the competition, and we *lose* money!

The "Yes but . . ." Winner's Curse Rizzutoism

Yet, companies do this all the time. Why? The spirit of competition prompts them to justify it on various grounds: "there will be follow-on business" or "there are strategic reasons for being in that market" or "we need to round out our portfolio or product line." This is merely another Rizzutoism in practice, something I call the "Yes but Winner's Curse Rizzutoism." It is a very slippery slope; we are in business to *make money*—not lose money in the short term and (hopefully, possibly) eventually make it back at some unspecified date in the future. If you are going to make the argument that this particular deal will lead to follow-on business, then you had better come prepared with a solid case. That is, provide specific company names and contact people, the exact dollar amount of revenue and margins (often I find that the follow-on business also loses money), dates when this will be booked and revenue collected, the exact present value of these future cash flows in today's dollars, all weighed against the loss incurred today and adjusted for the risk and uncertainty of actually booking this follow-on business. Only with this information can we construct a justified business case for whether booking a loss now makes sense. And I rarely, if ever, see this in practice. And that's too bad, since customers use it to their advantage all the time (I would).

How to Avoid the "Yes but" Winner's Curse Rizzutoism

1. Require business case justification.
2. Eliminate the phrase "Yes, but . . ."
3. Mandate financial evaluation of strategic decisions, including:
   - adjustments for the present value of future cash flows
   - expected (not hoped for) margins
   - the probability of actually booking the future business
   - the risk associated with present versus future financial flows
4. Examine portfolio needs rigorously using appropriate financial tools and metrics.
5. Let your people know this is required; this alone will prevent the vast majority of "Yes but" Rizzutoisms from even being brought forward in the first place.

How to Take Advantage of the "Yes but" Winner's Curse Rizzutoism

A Fortune 500 CEO once told his senior sales executives during an all-day strategy session that once they've gotten to a line review, that is, a major customer bringing all major suppliers into a single location to compete for its business, they've already lost. He was right. A buyer wants simultaneous competition and bidding, and you should do whatever you can to facilitate this for all of the reasons noted earlier. A seller, on the other hand, wants to avoid this at all costs. Once you've arrived in that building for the line review, supplier conference, whatever mask they want to put on it, you've already lost.

Points of Access—Strategic Barriers to Entry and the Story of Blockbuster

For Captain Pollard, the (unfounded) fear of the cannibals on the Marquesas blocked effective access to the optimal solution to the crew's dilemma. In business, there are countless examples of the use of creative entry barriers in the economics literature,[9] but two recent ones—involving Apple and Amazon—stand out for their strategic use of the principle of the value chain discussed earlier. Think back to Chapter 4's discussion about how Apple and Amazon strategically use their control of the value chain from back to front to gain advantage. In order to place some of this in context, we need to go back in history a bit, too—perhaps to the firm that executed a similar approach to perfection, namely Blockbuster.[10]

Blockbuster was one of the early entrants into the video rental market right at the time when VCRs began to gain traction.[11] The market in these early days was much like the wild west of video technology, a lesson in facing uncertainty in technological change. It was a time when the most powerful man in Hollywood was none other than Mr. Fred Rogers of kids' show *Mr. Rogers' Neighborhood* fame,[12] and where the leading and best technology, Betamax, ultimately lost the battle to dominate the market. This was also true of the video rental market where local mom and pop operators were often the first to open a store in a local market, gaining a loyal following of customers who rented their favorite titles from the store down the road. Enter Blockbuster, whose CEO was used to tough battles in the waste management industry.

Blockbuster's strategy was one of stocking deep and "co-locating" near—and thereby bankrupting—the prevailing local mom and pop store. This tactic relied on Blockbuster's growth and ability to manage inventory, thereby utilizing that growth in ways with which the local stores simply couldn't compete.

But what exactly does this mean—and why did it drive the locals out of the market virtually without exception? One key issue for video store operators in the early days was managing inventory. Each week, there was high demand for the hot new titles; but after a few weeks, new became old, and the demand for the formerly sought-after titles subsided in a predictably dramatic fashion. Local operators—that typically had one to three stores in their market—couldn't stock too deeply on the most current titles. If they did, they'd be stuck with a large inventory of movies that wouldn't rent once they dropped off in popularity over time. Hence, the local operators attempted to manage hot titles in a variety of ways. One of these was to allocate a limited supply across customers, which invariably left a number of customers, who could not rent the titles they wanted, unhappy.

Blockbuster didn't have this problem, and it knew it. It was growing rapidly and opening new stores daily. And it *could* stock deep, precisely *because* of its growth. When one Blockbuster store had excess inventory of a title that was no longer hot, it simply moved that inventory onto the shelves of a new store opening in order to stock that store's catalog inventory. While a local store would have to hold any title that they stocked deep, Blockbuster actually used these titles to lower the start-up costs of new store openings.

This provided Blockbuster with two distinct strategic advantages based on its growth: lower new store inventory costs and the ability to stock deep on the newest and hottest titles at any Blockbuster store. The second advantage was crucial, since demand at the local level knew nothing of this strategy. All they knew was that the mom and pop store down the block seemed to always be out of the most in-demand titles, whereas the Blockbuster right next door guaranteed that it would always have the newest and latest titles. In fact, Blockbuster knew that it had succeeded in driving the local store out of business "the minute the local store began putting up the 2-for-1-special signs."[13] The strategy was intentional; it was both brilliant and diabolical.

Note that a debate on the ethics of this approach, that is, intentionally driving out local businesses through sheer size and scale, misses the example's point, which is: an integrated strategy that recognizes the importance of scale and growth can be extraordinarily effective in gaining market share and precluding entry.

In this respect, the video market of today is, in many ways, fundamentally the same as that which Blockbuster faced in the early days of video. Specifically, competitors and collaborators such as Netflix; Redbox; Redbox/Verizon; cable companies such as Time Warner Cable, Comcast, AT&T; streaming video providers such as Hulu and Apple; content providers such as the movie theaters and television networks; and content distributors such as Amazon, Apple, Google, Barnes & Noble, and others, are all competing in what has become the Wild, Wild West of digital video transmission.

To appreciate some of the issues at hand, it's illustrative to watch Netflix's business model evolve through necessity. Netflix had a significant impact on the demise of Blockbuster through an innovative business model—physically distributing DVDs through the mail at low cost and high availability. It was able to do so thanks to its well defined lead times vis-à-vis the ordering process; that is, it could effectively predict and manage disc demand. While Netflix used mail distribution to erode Blockbuster's base, the cable providers nibbled at the company via digital downloads: Apple via a marginal Apple TV and more successful iTunes store, Internet content from YouTube to Hulu via Internet streaming, and Redbox (the DVD rental kiosks located at many supermarkets and Walmarts, etc.) by stealing share with an innovative approach of its own. It's easy to understand Blockbuster's business model's demise with the benefit of hindsight; the real question is how it wasn't apparent to Blockbuster sooner so that they could avoid their ultimate fate. In today's world, the innovative models of Netflix and Redbox—ones where distribution and content could provide an entry barrier much like "stocking deep" could to Blockbuster many years ago—will doubtlessly give way to video streaming. Physical distribution is no longer necessary; therefore, the question for content providers/distributors is how to create barriers to entry when all it takes is a website and agreement to distribute. Can someone make money in a world that is *contestable* (see William J. Baumol, John C. Panzar, and Robert D. Willig, *Contestable Markets and the Theory of Industry Structure*, Harcourt, 1982) with extraordinarily low entry barriers?

The key lies in any one player's ability to gain advantage through strategic control points in the value chain. Netflix is trying to do this by generating its own content. Social game service provider Zynga is an excellent example of a company that was able to do this effectively. Facebook's Farmville distribution played an instrumental role in giving Zynga strategic control of access to prime gaming customers in a world where word-of-mouth grows exponentially. The Facebook connection for Zynga was brilliant. Absent a similar vehicle to exclude simultaneous choice across streaming platforms, the ability to make money for any video distributor—be it Netflix, Redbox, Blockbuster or a new entrant—is unlikely at best.

As we move into the future, strategic control points may be mobile distribution exclusivity. Redbox's agreement with Verizon brings up an interesting value chain strategic possibility. If a content distributor such as Redbox, Blockbuster, Apple, Netflix (or even an entirely new entrant) aligned exclusively with a mobile data or home Internet provider, it could give Netflix or Redbox a huge strategic control point. We can even take this one step further and apply the "Amazon model": were they to find a way to align back to front in the entertainment value chain with content creators (studios, networks, etc.), these customers would gain a substantial strategic advantage. In short, the only thing that will save Netflix, Redbox and other content distributors from being anything other than a commodity is control over the value chain—something Amazon and Apple realized a long time ago in digital publishing.

So, how have the traditional content distributors fought back? A classic and effective approach is the use of bundling, taking advantage of the strategic control point noted previously. Cable providers such as Time Warner Cable, Comcast, and AT&T have realized that Internet access is crucial. Once they bundle this with other services such as television and IP-based phone service, access to the house provides a strategic advantage that other rivals cannot match. The result is higher revenue per house, lower individual-level demand elasticity and, with price lock guarantees, barriers to entry.[14]

Points of Touch—The Embodiment of Your Strategy

Imagine the following scenario. You are searching for a new pair of shoes to buy, and you want to know what the major brands are and where to buy them. You first consult your Yellow Pages book and then sit by the television waiting for advertisements for shoes and shoe stores.

Do you know anyone who would do either of those things today? Of course not. Rather than waiting for information to be pushed to you via television and other media, you *seek it out*. Today's communication strategies are about getting the information out to multiple points of touch and letting the customer seek out the most efficient and relevant avenues for them.

Following the process just described should lead you to a fairly obvious communications tactic, which should be the embodiment of a firm's strategy. Once you know which high-priority segments you're targeting, have conducted a detailed analysis of their underlying attribute needs, know how your offering is better than those of competitors, then the messaging should be clear.

In the old days, companies would devise this message, create a communications plan with their advertising agency and/or media planner and push it out to potential customers through a pre-designed plan via various media channels. Today, we no longer control much of what happens; users pull in information via a website, a web search, or some other avenue (Google knows everything).

Research in the media environment has found, for example, that there's a significant economic value added by separating out and targeting individuals.[15] Further, in an era of big data, those companies that are better at reaching multiple points of touch will ultimately be the winners precisely because customers today *seek out information*. If your offering isn't in the outlet (such as Internet search results, blogs, billboards, and so on) that they search, you will be excluded from consideration. Big data is about how to make information available.

Points of touch matter today. You can't control the process; you can only get what you want out to the right places and let the rest take its course. It's a control freak's nightmare—but it's the world in which we live.

Chapter Summary and Key Business Principles

- A fear of the unknown can lead us to the presumed safety of what is known, often with disastrous consequences.

- Research and access to information is crucial.

- Lack of information is not, in and of itself, a reason to disregard a strategic option.

- The opportunity cost of taking only known strategic alternatives can be high. Do not limit the set of options you consider to what is known.

- Sometimes fear of the cannibals should be your last concern. Cannibalize your own sales before someone else does.

- Tactics today are about a new paradigm, the Five Points of Effective Tactics outlined above:

  o Points in positioning: Position around strategic control points, emphasizing attributes that give customers a reason to buy.

  o Points in time: First-mover advantage around a strategic control point can be real, lasting, and sustainable; those around attributes are usually fleeting.

○ Points of value: To extract value today, think and plan for competitive response (Heinz), anticipate competitive moves (card example) and beware the "winner's curse."

○ Points of access: Strategic barriers of entry through control points (Blockbuster example).

○ Points of touch: How you touch your customers through multiple venues (such as physical points of sale, Internet, social media, and so on).

Key Business Tools

- Strategic use of information
- Data mining and analytics (big data)
- Leveraging strategic control points
- Incentive alignment
- Winner's Curse
- Five Points of Effective Tactics

What Is So Different about Today? Conclusions and Lessons for the Future

Leveraging this Knowledge for Strategic Advantage—Conclusions and Directions Forward
                    —The Story of the Multiple Listing Service,
                              the U.S. Supreme Court,
                    the U.S. Department of Justice and Redfin

H ave you ever bought or sold a home or any real estate? If you answered yes, the following story should sound familiar. You work with an agent who plays all roles, from finding listings and showing you a house to negotiating on your behalf. For this service, the agent receives a fixed fee as a percent of the sales price no matter what they do or how good or bad the service they perform. Thus, we begin with an almost century-old convention—the 6 percent real estate commission and multiple listing service.

Real estate brokers, who have earned a fixed fee of 6 percent of the purchase price for the past 70 years, typically facilitate the buying and selling of real estate. This standard commission amount came into being in the 1940s when the local Realtor boards openly colluded on rates. The U.S. Supreme Court declared in the 1950s that this was in violation of antitrust laws, so the Realtors adopted "suggested fees." Then in the 1970s, Department of Justice lawsuits banned the suggested fees as well, so the Realtors made the commissions implicit. Numerous studies found that the real estate commission in the United States remained at 6 percent for decades, while 3.5 percent is a more typical commission structure internationally.[1] The primary reason? The Realtors have had ownership of an exclusive strategic control point: the multiple listing service (MLS).

The MLS is a suite of services that enable real estate brokers to share and coordinate property-listing information, among other tasks. Most MLS systems have historically restricted membership and access to Realtors. These agents are appropriately licensed by the state and have steadfastly refused to give up control of the listing to external sources. Indeed, the National Association of Realtors (NAR) had set restrictive policies that permit brokers to show only limited MLS information on their websites under a system known as IDX or Internet Data Exchange. However, in 2005, the U.S. Department of Justice filed an antitrust lawsuit against the NAR over its policy of restricting certain online brokers from displaying MLS information. The case was settled in May 2008, with NAR agreeing that Internet brokerages would be given access to all the same listings that traditional brokerages are.[2]

Enter Redfin.com.

In the traditional home-buying process, the agent would do the research based on the client's requirements and show him or her a list of houses (either printed on paper or e-mailed as links to the MLS listing site) with all the detailed information. The client would then select a number of homes to tour with the agent, who would arrange for such tours. If the client decides to make an offer on a home, the agent would then pull recent comparable sale listings or "comps," and devise an offer package based on the comps. The agent would then present the offer to the seller's agent, who, in turn, would present it to the owner. It is then up to the owner to either accept or reject the offer. If the offer is accepted, the home goes "under contract."

There is a list of tasks with which your agent may or may not assist you, including obtaining financing, ordering inspections, reading disclosures, removing contingencies, and so on, but whatever he or she ends up doing, the agent controls the process and information *every step of the way*. As a buyer or seller, your agent is your sole portal to what is happening with the transaction, precisely as the NAR would like.

So, what's so different about the Redfin model—and how does this turn the traditional real estate market on its head?

The Redfin business model splits the tasks of the traditional agent into distinct areas of responsibility. It compensates the agent at each stage based on customer satisfaction metrics and rebates a portion of the commission back to the buyer (see Figure 9.1). More specifically, Redfin shifts the research responsibilities to the homebuyer, a.k.a., the client. The Redfin website is able to display all properties listed on MLS, updated in real time. Clients can therefore do their own research on the houses that they may want to view or make an offer on. When the client is ready for a tour, she clicks a button, and a Redfin tour coordinator contacts her by phone or e-mail. The tour coordinator puts the client in touch with a home tour agent— someone who specializes in home tours *only* and does not offer other services. When the client is ready to make an offer, she clicks a button on the website. At this point, a Redfin offer coordinator will contact her to put her in touch with an offer agent. The offer agent does nothing but write up offers, and is therefore highly specialized in this area. What this means is that this Redfin offer agent spends a lot more time examining comps and researching pricing than a traditional agent does. Once the buyer accepts an offer, Redfin offers a checklist and corresponding deadlines of all the tasks that the client will complete. Both the tour agent and the offer agent are licensed real estate agents. Redfin pays them on a salary basis with the option of a bonus that is solely tied to a client satisfaction survey. Since the agents are not paid on commission, Redfin is able to refund the client up to 50 percent of the buyer agent's commission.[3]

The refund is a key differentiator for the homebuyer and signals the beginning of the erosion of the commission structure. For a client who doesn't mind doing her own research, there is a sample list of the approximate refund that she may get based on a range of home purchase prices; these are significant:

Purchase Price	$500,000	$750,000	$1,000,000	$1,250,000	$1,500,000
Rebate to buyer	$6,250	$9,375	$12,500	$15,625	$18,750

The idea of bringing a traditional brokerage online isn't new; it happened long ago in the finance and investment world with the

Phases	Traditional	Redfin
Research	Agent	Client
Tour	Agent, Client	Tour Coordinator, Tour Agent, Client
Offer	Agent, Client	Offer Coordinator, Offer Agent, Client
Contract-pending Task List	Client (Agent help)	Client
Commission Refund	None	$$$

Figure 9.1   The Redfin Model versus the Traditional Real Estate Agent Model at Each Stage of the Buying Process

online brokerage firms. Indeed, investment discount brokerages have been operating on the Internet since the 1990s, driving trading commission down from hundreds of dollars to today's sub-$10 range. One can be sure that the same will happen to the real estate brokerage commissions.

The major change in the real estate market is that the once tightly held strategic control point—the exclusive MLS listing service that *only Realtors* could historically access—is now openly accessible via the Internet. And while companies like Redfin.com are one group of beneficiaries, so, too, are homebuyers; we have already seen a change in the commission structure, now closer to 5 percent in most markets as a result.

Redfin was not the first to take advantage of such an opening. Online real estate database Zillow.com was around long before Redfin came on the scene. What is making Redfin a more likely winner is its new business model. By separating individual tasks in the home buying process and providing buyers with agents who are highly specialized in these fields, it enhances process efficiency. Furthermore, the licensed agents that Redfin hires are compensated by low salaries combined with the potential of bonuses solely based on client feedbacks, which goes a long way to ensuring client satisfaction.

Factors Driving Redfin's Success

- Releasing of the strategic control point of the MLS onto the Internet.
- Attracting homebuyers with attractive commission refunds.
- Shifting research and contract-pending project tasks toward the client to increase process efficiency.
- Separating transaction tasks to create highly specialized agents to increase process efficiency.
- Promoting client satisfaction by offering bonuses solely based on client satisfaction survey.

Bottom line: 70 years of sustained 6 percent real estate commission structure is now being eroded because the *key strategic control point has been opened up*. And this, in turn, has spawned a new business model that is fundamentally changing the residential real estate business right before our eyes.

Remember Blockbuster founder Wayne Huizenga's statement that he knew his company had succeeded in driving the local store out of business "the minute [they] began putting up the 2-for-1-special signs"? The same is true here: the erosion of the 6 percent commission to 5 percent and now 5 percent minus the Redfin rebate represents the same phenomenon. Expect commissions to continue to fall closer to the international average of 3.5 percent now that the strategic control point has been opened up to all.

So, what can we learn from this? What is so different about today?

Speed

Figure 9.2 shows the time it took various products to reach a 40 percent penetration rate in the United States: telephone (1892), personal computer (1981), mobile phone (1987), Internet (1991) and smartphone (2001), with the approximate year of introduction in parentheses. What is clear is that the speed of adoption has been increasing over time (also see "Big Bang Disruption," *Harvard Business Review*, March 2013).

We live in an environment where tech darling Apple launched the iPhone in November 2007 and the original iPad in April 2010. Nowadays, the two products account for more than 70 percent of Apple's revenue—showing that markets can evolve at lightning speed, as Figure 9.2 suggests. Those slow to react can be decimated; as noted earlier, BlackBerry had more smartphone sales than Apple

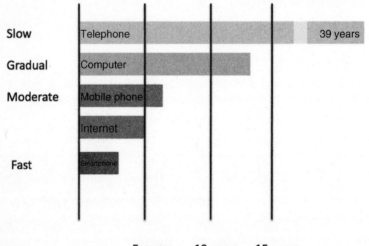

Figure 9.2   Time from 10 Percent to 40 Percent Penetration
Note: Tablets are omitted, having achieved the 10 percent threshold in 2011.

Source: www.phonearena.com.

and Samsung combined just four years ago. Now it has less than 5 percent market share. If you worked for Verizon or Time Warner Cable 4 or 5 years ago, would you have thought then that your main competitor in the near future would be that "search engine" company Google?! What is particularly different is that this isn't unique to technology products. The speed of accessing information has changed virtually every industry on the planet—and those that haven't changed appreciably already represent opportunities for others to step in and facilitate that change.

Interconnectedness

Since the dawn of television in the 1940s, advertisers have pushed information to viewers in the form of television advertisements. Today, what is more common is talk about a "second screen"—your iPhone or smartphone, your iPad or tablet, that you have with you while you watch your favorite show or team. Internet-enabled televisions, DVD players, and devices like Apple TV and TiVo have transformed our viewing experiences and led advertisers to focus on the whole experience of getting information to us by taking advantage of our proclivity for seeking out (Googling) information. The interconnectedness of our computer to our smartphone to our television—even to our cars these days—means that what we do in one place carries with us to the next. It has transformed an advertising business that had remained virtually static for some three-quarters of a century—and it has transformed both how we get information and the efficiency of getting this information in the first place.

Similarly, Google's new Project Glass discussed in the introduction to this book is one example of how interconnectedness plays out in today's markets. Recall that Google connects every offering through the Google glasses that utilize an always on, ubiquitous wireless connection. Even this has started to give way to new technologies such as moving images imbedded into your contact lenses, "spray on WiFi" capabilities to facilitate distribution of WiFi signals (see, for example, www.telegraph.co.uk/technology/news/9729403/Text-messages-direct-to-your-contact-lens.html and www.wired.com/business/2013/01/ff-seven-big-ideas/3), and the like. Examples of information interconnectedness and how it's being used nowadays are countless and varied: war is being transformed by the coordination of assets involving "integrated battle space" and control of home systems is being interconnected. Every piece of the value chain, every point of access, every point of touch can now be connected. Those that use this interconnectedness to their advantage are the ones that will win in today's environment.

Ubiquity (Mobile)

We now take our information and therefore this interconnectedness with us wherever we go. Smartphones, tablets, cars, planes, trains, and homes—and soon enough, our watches, glasses, and contact lenses—mean we are always on the grid no matter where we are or how fast we're traveling.

Always On

This is similar to ubiquity in that it also draws on the concept that connectivity to information is universal. We access information no matter what time of day or day of the week. This introduces the possibility for revolutionary changes that many haven't even contemplated. I discussed Google's Project Glass in a session I was leading at the Yale Law School this past year on corporate governance. I spoke specifically of how companies' ability access to this always-on Internet during meetings (and possibly broadcast live!) will present issues that they've never faced before. For example: what if a disgruntled meeting attendee broadcasts sensitive or confidential board meeting topics? I would argue that the key for governance is incentives. You can't eliminate the always-on culture through rules alone. You need to make it such that those in the meeting have *no incentive* to broadcast sensitive information in the first place, because there is simply no way to prevent such behavior through rules. The always-on nature of information is affecting us in ways that span personal privacy to corporate strategy, tactics, and incentives. It is truly a different world.

The New Math of Today's Business Environment

$Speed + Interconnectedness + Ubiquity\,(Mobile) + Always\,on = e^x$
   (Transformational change and exponential growth)

The Information Revolution of the 1990s has finally taken hold in ways that most of us never imagined. It's the combination of information, the Internet, and the ubiquitous, always-on and interconnectedness of what we do today that has fundamentally changed the name of the game in strategy for old-school and new technology companies alike.

Conclusion: We're all old.

The sea change we see in business today is not limited to high-technology markets. Owens Corning operates in old-line industries that have been around for many years. Its core is producing products made from glass fibers—reinforcements, insulation, shingles and roofing materials, and related building and composite materials (its two divisions are the Building Materials Group and Composites). But doing work in an old-line industry does not necessarily mean functioning in the backwater. In fact, Owens Corning is led by a young, forward-looking, and articulate CEO by the name of Mike Thaman. While operating on the bottom rankings of the Fortune

500 and having come through bankruptcy in the wake of asbestos liability, the company has developed a rigor to its approach to strategy incorporating game theory, choice analysis, detailed channel pricing data, and demand/regression analysis. It has pushed these customer insights down into the field to better equip the sales teams that work there. We can learn quite a bit from Owens Corning's progressive approach to customer interaction, but perhaps it makes more sense to examine the source of its approach to the market: the success of others.

As in many of the examples in this book, Owens Corning's senior leaders learn from watching others. It's a trait virtually all successful companies share. To this end, we conclude with a Top 10 list of observations for operating in what is truly the age of information—observations that we can take from industry today.

1. *We're all old.* I had a telling experience while presenting to a group of corporate leaders at a presentation at Yale University recently. When the subject of Google's Project Glass came up, one senior board member in his 50s spoke up to let me know that he was concerned. He worried specifically that while someone was watching the heads-up display on the glasses for video or weather updates, he might walk into a busy street into oncoming traffic and get hit by a car or a bus. I immediately thought of the woman who fell into a fountain at a mall while staring at her BlackBerry. Interestingly, there was one young woman in her early 20s who raised her hand and said that her first reaction was "No, I thought just the opposite, maybe this device could *warn* me *before* I am about to get hit by a car!" The two reactions—one from a 50-something and the other from a 20-something—were very revealing. If you're over 30—and probably if you're past your early 20s—then you're old. In today's environment (and particularly in the future environment), the reaction of today's youth will dominate. If you're looking for trends and future disruptive technologies,

look no further than demographics and the attitudes and perspective of the young.

2. *Incentives, incentives, incentives.* You can't control any more. There are the legendary stories of Andrew Carnegie and the United States Steel Corporation and how U.S. corporate leaders led with an iron fist—this as a way to lead can work no longer. Between the ability to share information instantly and anonymously, to whistle-blower laws, to badly misaligned incentives between management and the average worker in U.S. companies today, mandating behavior— especially company loyalty—is now next to impossible. Incentivizing this through stock ownership, vested pensions, board transparency, and the like are the only way to govern in this age of instant information and gratification.

3. *Points of access.* Distribution was the old-line term about how we physically got product from factory to retailer to end customer. Today, being effective is about giving your customer—be it in the channel such as with a big box retailer like Home Depot or the end user—multiple routes to your offering. These multiple routes can include the Internet and direct delivery, traditional retail, network marketing, you name it. The key is allowing customers to get to your product in the way *they prefer* to maximize the probability that they will choose your product, while simultaneously incentivizing them to access *you* through the most efficient means possible. A bank, for example, would rather you do business online or through a smartphone than via an ATM; however, it would prefer you visit an ATM than spend time with one of its tellers. The bottom line: allow multiple points of access and incentivize to the right one for your business.

4. *Points of touch.* The traditional way to communicate was to do a large media buy on network television or through a major publisher. Today, businesses have no such control. We can

push all we want, but the social networks will dominate in the end (particularly for offerings dependent upon repeat sales). Therefore, our financial success will critically depend upon how well we manage the incentives to encourage optimal customer behavior.

5. *Creative destruction and trend alignment.* By all rights, Sony should have won the MP3 war, as discussed earlier. Only a true psychic—and perhaps Steve Jobs—would have predicted that it would be Apple *Computer.* Many of the trends that we see today—alternative materials, information interconnectivity, information security, the intelligent use of big data—are, in my view, obvious. Unfortunately, we are all too close to our own industries to see the inevitability of our own demise. Often today we're so concerned with Big Data that we miss the Big Picture. Shift happens; ignore it at your peril.

6. *Order matters.* This is particularly true with respect to strategic control in the value chain. We often focus—incorrectly—on first and early moves into a new *product* space, such as failures like the Apple Newton or successes like the iPod. Unfortunately, this means that we often *fail* to see the value chain, strategic control, and infrastructure necessary for success. The iPod succeeded in large part *not* because it was early to market, but because the infrastructure was in place (the same can be said about the iPhone launch) and because Apple controlled the value chain. Be first and early to dominate in an area based on product features and this will often be easily imitated; be first and early to dominate in an area based on strategic control points in the value chain and you can use this to dominate others in the product space. New introductions that focus on attributes, features or the product without concern for points of strategic control all too often lead to early product introductions that are easily imitated, easily improved upon, or simply just not good enough. Lead with the

value chain; control the critical parts of the value chain first and foremost.

7. *Type A, obsessive-compulsive and controlling personalities beware.* Admittedly, I am one of these. I want to control every aspect of a business of which I am part to ensure it is done right. The world in which we live today is anything but conducive to control. We have power over less and less of what happens—and the sooner we realize that, the better. We can't manage social media, control information, or prevent data leakage; we cannot govern and lead via regulation anymore. We can only incentivize behavior that is consistent with the objectives that we want. That makes the likes of me exceedingly uncomfortable, but I, and others like me, must live with it, recognize it, and deal with it. It is the way of the world today.

8. *Think ahead.* I've discussed this in detail throughout the book. Yet I am always amazed how often companies wait and see what the competitors do first. Why? You will always know what their strategic options are, and you will know which one of those will be better for you and which ones will not be. Why in the world wouldn't you want to influence those outcomes by changing your rival's incentive structure by putting a stake in the ground first?

9. *Follow the money.* Rigidly prioritize. Use the Willie Sutton rule; use whatever makes it happen. Good companies have a single-minded obsession with following the money. Enough said.

10. *Think like a 20-year-old.* For many of us, this has to be the hardest one. Note that it really should have read "think like a 17- or 18-year-old," but I thought I'd be kind to those of us who have been around for a while and for whom thinking like a 20-year-old sounds however slightly more reasonable and palatable.

Think ahead. Order matters. Follow the money. Incentivize, don't govern. Destroy constructively. Think like a 20-year-old. If you don't, you will be behind—in the metaphorical tail of the comet.

Good luck taking the tools, processes and, most important, way of thinking captured in this book, forward to business success. Get prepared for a wild ride—the future will only intensify the issues raised here. I can't imagine a more exciting time to be in business.

NOTES

Introduction

1. See "Nokia's Bad Call on Smartphones" in the *Wall Street Journal*, July 2012: http://online.wsj.com/article/SB1000142405 2702304388004577531002591315494.html.

2. The direct quote is "Nowadays the only true consumer marketers are retailers—and forward integrated manufacturers with their own retail capabilities—because these have the transactional relationship with the consumer. But even retailers—as customers of wholesalers and manufacturers—are players in B2B markets." Source: personal correspondence, March 18, 2013.

3. *Time*, February 11, 2013, page 16.

Chapter 1   The Importance of Fundamentals

1. Robert Frank, *Choosing the Right Pond: Human Behavior and the Quest for Status* (New York: Cambridge University Press, 1985), 3.

2. To reinforce this example, the Driver and Vehicle Licensing Agency in the United Kingdom once did a survey of British drivers that asked, "Do you believe that you are an average, above average, or below average driver?" It turns out that 98 percent of British drivers believe that they are above average!

3. A detailed account is provided in the book *Barbarians at the Gate: The Fall of RJR Nabisco* by Bryan Burrough and John Helyar (New York: Harper Business, 2009 [reprint edition]).

4. See Harvard Business School case 9–801–361, "Howard Schulz and Starbucks Coffee Company."

5. Attribute-based willingness to pay models originating in Lancaster's work from the 1960s provides the theoretical underpinnings of conjoint analysis, originally proposed by Paul Green in 1964. These "stated preference" models (including choice analysis (Louviere, et al. 2000) and conjoint analysis (see, e.g., Green and Srinivasan 1990)) and, to a lesser degree, "revealed preference" models such as Hedonic analysis (Rosen 1974), are used quite often in consumer markets. In this book, we make the connection to the validity of using these approaches in a B2B setting, as well.

6. *Stated Choice Methods: Analysis and Applications*, Jordan J. Louviere, David A. Hensher, Joffre D. Swait, and Wiktor Adamowicz, Cambridge University Press, 2000; Paul E. Green and V. Srinivasan, "Conjoint Analysis in Marketing: New Developments with Implications for Research and Practice," *Journal of Marketing* 54 (4), October 1990, 3–19; Sherwin Rosen, "Hedonic Prices and Implicit Markets: Product Differentiation in Pure Competition," *Journal of Political Economy* 82 (1), January–February 1974, 34–55.

7. The concept of *core competencies* is defined as the unique ability that a company possesses that cannot be easily imitated, such as automotive assembly technology, design, or printer technology as in the two examples here.

8. The process as outlined is sequential and linear, as in a flow diagram. In practice, the process is anything but sequential and linear. If done properly, each of the earlier steps is reviewed constantly throughout the process. Engineers and scientists often feel unsettled with the looseness of the process, which

is part art and part science. Part of the intent of this book is to provide the foundation in science to allow the art to shine through—thinking out of the box within the frame of the box.

9. The process is one that has been developed over almost 25 years of working with Fortune 500 companies around the world, bringing in the best of corporate practice as well as the best of models and approaches used by leading consulting companies and academics. See www.ChestnutHillConsulting.com and www.CADEOEconomics.com.

10. Although actually misattributed, famous bank robber Willie Sutton was quoted as saying that he robbed banks because "that's where the money is!"

11. Source of the Tesco example details: personal conversations, London, July 2000; Peapod, initially launched in Chicago, is one good relative success story in the United States. For a detailed analysis of Webvan and Tesco, see Kelly Delaney-Klinger, Kenneth K. Boyer, and Mark Frohlich, "The return of online grocery shopping: a comparative analysis of Webvan and Tesco's operational methods," *The TQM Journal* 15 (3), 2003, 187–196.

Chapter 2 Finding the Right Market Opportunities

1. Credit to Ben Robinson for the original version of this (made up) story.

2. Source: http://en.wikipedia.org/wiki/Self_checkout.

3. Source, all figures in this section: 2005 calendar year, from Time, Inc. and industry sources.

4. Source: Stores.org.

5. Sources: http://en.wikipedia.org/wiki/MP3.com throughout this section on MP3.com, in addition to www.mp3newswire.net/

stories/2000/riaavmp3.html and http://en.wikipedia.org/wiki/
UMG_v._MP3.com addressing the legal aspect of the lawsuit.

6. All from personal experience, including current Minidisc
ownership.

Chapter 3   Managing the Risk of Growth

1. Jeppesen figures, details and story used by express written permission of Jeppesen, January 2013.

2. Figures and intuition from Michael Collins, Marc André Kamel,
and Kristine Miller, "Growing Beyond Your Core in Retail" (Bain
& Company, 2006) and Chris Zook, "Increasing the Odds of
Successful Growth: The Critical Prelude to Moving 'Beyond the
Core,'" *Strategy and Leadership* 32, no. 4 (2004), 17–23; or see
Chris Zook and James Allen, "Growth Outside the Core,"
Harvard Business Review, December 2003.

3. See   http://en.wikipedia.org/wiki/Connexion_by_Boeing   for
more detail on Connexion by Boeing and www.forbes.com/
sites/chunkamui/2011/04/15/dissecting-ciscos-flip-flop/ for more
detail on Cisco's "Flip Flop on Flip" (quote from article).

4. Much of the narrative taken from Jeppesen's web page (www
.jeppesen.com), internal Jeppesen communications and videos at
Jeppesen.com   (http://ww1.jeppesen.com/educational/jeppesen-
charts-video.jsp).

Chapter 4   Choosing and Competing Effectively in the Right Space

1. Philip H. Dougherty, "$6 Million to Back Minnetonka's
Softsoap." *New York Times*, February 5, 1980, D15.

2. We will focus on the industry supply chain here in order to
understand the impact of competition and the competitive game

being played throughout the supply chain and across markets. In contrast, at the firm level, the concept of value chain analysis was developed by Porter in 1985 to assist efforts in "following the money" throughout the firm's chain of operations and, as such, is inward looking rather than market facing. In its simplest form, it creates a flow of value creation from the input of raw materials on through to delivery, service, and support of the final offering in the market. As it was originally conceived, an organization can be divided into separate processes or functions as value is created. These were divided into five primary activities and four secondary activities. Primary activities include inbound logistics, operations, outbound logistics, marketing/sales, and service and support. Secondary activities include things like firm infrastructure (general management, planning, finance, legal), human resource management, technology development, and procurement.

3. Jeppesen figures, details, and story used by expressed written permission from Jeppesen, January 2013.

4. The rest of the value chain (software, route planning, GUI, etc.), Jeppesen could produce as well or better than any other software company. While software and route planning were core competencies of Jeppesen, they were not strategic control points: Jeppesen creating this software did not prevent any other company *with access to the data* from doing the same thing. By contrast, if one firm owned the data or bridge access exclusively, this would indeed prevent any rival from competing. This illustrates the key difference between a core competency and a strategic control point.

5. It is important to note that there are many nuances that make the issues at hand more complex than represented here. For example, it is possible to enter with route optimization without chart data (as OSI did in part); indeed, Jeppesen Marine currently offers route optimization and navigation products separately. Further, although official data was largely owned by the UKHO, since in

2005 only paper charts were *required*, access to official charts only became a critical issue as the ECDIS digital mandate kicks in in stages starting in 2013.

Chapter 5   Targeting the Right Customers in the Right Space with the Right Offering

1. *Time* magazine, March 18, 2013.
2. This quote is folklore. Apparently, it was a reporter that made the quote up, but it has been attributed to Willie Sutton ever since.
3. Note that "mass customization" pioneered by Dell and others is another way to get the best of both worlds. By limiting choice on the bespoke parts to only those critical parts of the offering (we don't choose the mother board or the chip manufacturer or the color of the wires in a Dell computer, for example), some manufacturers are able to gain scale while customizing and tailoring the offering to the needs of the individual customer.
4. See Ted Levitt's classic article, "The Globalization of Markets," *Harvard Business Review*, May/June 1983, 92–102.
5. Many thanks to Cam Tipping, President and Founder of IIBD (International Institute for Business Development, www.iibd.com, world leader in business simulation software (SABRE)), for the story told here.
6. Source: www.Nike.com and CNBC special report *Nike*.
7. Source: www.about.com.
8. Source for data: American Express, Visa, and MasterCard annual reports.
9. For an outstanding technical treatment, see Kamakura and Wedel, *Market Segmentation* (Hoboken, NJ: John Wiley & Sons, 2005).

10. "Strong Apple Shipments Drive Robust Tablet Market Growth in Second Quarter, According to IDC," IDC press release, August 2, 2012, www.idc.com/getdoc.jsp?containerId=prUS23632512.

Chapter 6   Understanding Your Customers in the Right Space

1. Harvard Business School case study #9–500–068, "Coca-Cola's New Vending Machine (A): Pricing to Capture Value, or Not?"; UNC Kenan-Flagler decision experiments, October 2012.

2. Relevant comments by Dan Ariely, a Duke Fuqua School professor, on BigThink.com (bigthink.com/ideas/20748) provide accurate, timely, and helpful thoughts on this subject.

3. Quote from an interesting presentation by Ken Schmidt, former head of branding at Harley Davidson, at the WDUnleash conference, Chicago, November 2012.

4. We refer to the common "conjoint analysis" under the broader heading of "choice analysis" recognizing that many industry researchers, particularly those in packaged goods industries, understand the potential power of conjoint analysis. Choice analysis is the more general heading we use here since it refers to a broader class of models that use not only the experimental design techniques employed by conjoint analysis, but detailed economic models of choice theory, strongly preferred from both a theoretical and practical standpoint.

5. Technically, the trade-offs are presented using "orthogonal" designs so that there is a forced trade-off between attributes that allows us to statistically assess the incremental impact of the inclusion (or exclusion) of any attribute. The technique has its origins in the hard sciences where orthogonal designs are used to isolate the effect of treatment versus control, as in cancer research.

6. Traditionally, such analysis was conducted in aggregate—assessing overall consumer response in a market of 100 million customers, for example. Recent research has emphasized the ability of choice studies to assess individual choice trade-offs and decisions, making it particularly informative for those operating in a B2B environment.

7. We will use this simplest example here, noting that this is for illustration only and that the possibilities in terms of type of presentations are almost endless, ranging from the simple example below to elaborate studies using virtual reality or advanced statistical design techniques (our focus here is on what the approach can do in terms of customer insight rather than the nuanced details of implementation on the ground).

8. In addition, we are able to test the statistical significance of each level of each attribute. More formally, we can test the null hypothesis that each coefficient is equal to 0. If we cannot reject the (null) hypothesis that the coefficient is equal to zero, we can generally conclude that it is not material to Ashley's choice decision. Here, the only estimated coefficients that are statistically different than 0 are price (both $175 and $225) and ocean view. Hence, we conclude that the hotel brand name and the type of bed are not important factors in her hotel choice here.

9. This example is a true story, the names and players changed to protect confidentiality.

10. Note that, technically, the coordinates of each "dot" correspond to the estimated "coefficients" from the statistical analysis of the individual results (discussed earlier).

11. CADEO Economics has developed a proprietary, rigorous, and complex decision engine that combines choice theory, game theory, advanced optimization routines, and Bayesian updating to offer the only methodology available combining choice and game theory to provide both customer and competitive analysis. See www.CADEOEconomics.com for further details.

Chapter 7   Vertical Incentive Alignment and Asset Specificity

1. Much of the detail of this section comes from personal conversations with John Pepper at P&G during the early 1990 period, all occurring at the Yale School of Management.

2. Note that, largely for antitrust reasons, P&G was only able to obtain real-time information on its own products. Information on competitor products was obtained with the same 30-day lag as the competitors received their information.

3. This information was obtained via a personal conversation with John Pepper, P&G CEO, at the Yale School of Management in early 1992.

4. Credit for the term *asset specificity* is generally given to Oliver Williamson, who was awarded the Sveriges Riksbank Prize in Economic Sciences in memory of Alfred Nobel in 2009 for his work in the area of company behavior.

5. Source: personal conversations with Michael Ryan and others at Tom Ryan Distributing at the time.

6. This dual exclusivity requirement is the "dual" part of dual exclusive territorial monopoly term. The restrictions on long-time dealers has recently been relaxed in the wake of the Anheuser-Busch sale to allow dealers such as Tom Ryan to distribute other non-directly-competing brands such as smaller niche import beer products. Dual exclusive territorial monopolies are generally deemed to be illegal under U.S. antitrust law. However, the malt beverage industry has an explicit exemption to this rule—further, some states mandate dual exclusive territorial monopolies in the malt beverage industry, providing huge competitive advantages to the larger players in the industry, most notably Anheuser-Busch.

Chapter 8 Setting Tactics in Today's Environment

1. For a detailed account, read *In the Heart of the Sea: The Tragedy of the Whaleship Essex* by Nathaniel Philbrick (New York: Penguin, 2001).

2. Ernst Malstem and I were keynote speakers at the Marketing Institute of Ireland Conference in Dublin shortly after his book was published. He famously introducing himself as Ernst, one word, as in Cher or Madonna.

3. Technically, this is referred to as a "Marshallian" (after the economist Alfred Marshall who first suggested the construct in the 1920s) or "unilateral" (as if one firm could unilaterally raise or lower prices without engendering a response by its rivals) demand elasticity. The concept of a (point) demand elasticity in its most general form expressed the percentage change in quantity demanded divided by the percentage change in price. Here, the consulting firm specified a simple log-log form.

4. One can't even argue that Heinz would have benefited from category growth; for the most part, price cuts and promotions are a zero-sum game in this category resulting in either stealing share or stockpiling behavior (i.e., stealing share from future periods). Short of creating a winter storm, it is difficult to get consumers to consume more soup overall. To Heinz's credit, it was skeptical of the advice it was being given and brought in an external advisor (the author of this book), who recommended that the price recommendations be shelved (pun intended).

5. This example was originally created by Dixit and Nalebuff: Avinash K. Dixit and Barry J. Nalebuff, *Thinking Strategically: The Competitive Edge in Business, Politics and Everyday Life* (Norton, 1993). While the creation of scarcity is certainly important, it is only part of the story. The use of information can preempt the incentive to create scarcity not only here, but in practice as well.

6. As related work (Putsis and Sen, "Should NFL Blackouts be Banned," *Applied Economics*, 32, 2000) has demonstrated, misguided U.S. antitrust policy in certain industries has allowed such collusive behavior for antiquated reasons, to wit, the National Football League's blackout exemption to U.S. antitrust law.

7. See Richard Thaler, *The Winner's Curse: Paradoxes and Anomalies in Every Day Life* (New York: Free Press, 1992).

8. Source: personal observation 1997 to 2005 via work with Barclays Bank, Royal Bank of Scotland.

9. See, for example, Richard Schmalensee, "Entry Deterrence in the Ready-to-Eat Breakfast Cereal Industry," *Bell Journal of Economics*, The RAND Corporation, vol. 9(2), 1978, on the use of proliferation strategies to deter entry in the ready-to-eat breakfast cereal market.

10. This example, in part, reflects a story told by Wayne Huizenga, CEO of Blockbuster at the time, over lunch at Morey's when he visited Yale University back in the mid-1990s.

11. For an early history of this market, see James Lardner, *Fast Forward: Hollywood, the Japanese and the VCR Wars* (New York: Norton, 1987).

12. As claimed by the presiding federal judge in the famed Betamax case, see Lardner, *Fast Forward*, 270–271.

13. Direct quote from Wayne Huizenga, Yale University talk. Note that such a problem would be resolved by an efficient clearing market for inventory, but such a market was not well developed at this time, and, as the number of local mom and pop stores began to wane, developing such an efficient clearing market became less and less likely over time.

14. For recent research that demonstrates the effectiveness of bundling and the residential cable industry, see Timothy Derdenger and Vineet Kumar, "The Dynamic Effects of Bundling as a

Product Strategy," Harvard Business School Working Paper 12–043, November 2012.

15. See, for example, "Audience Characteristics and Bundling: A Hedonic Analysis of Advertising Rates," M. Koschat and W. Putsis, *Journal of Marketing Research* 39 (May 2002), 262–273.

Chapter 9   What Is So Different about Today? Conclusions and Lessons for the Future

1. Source: *International Real Estate Review*.

2. Source: Wikipedia, "Multiple Listing Service."

3. An exception happens in the state of Oregon, where the refund of real estate commission is prohibited by law.

INDEX